COMBINATION REFERENCE

A simple and orderly arrangement of selected references to the Standard Works of the Church of Jesus Christ of Latter-day Saints

Prepared by

ELDIN RICKS

Published by

DESERET BOOK COMPANY

1952

ACKNOWLEDGMENTS

The writer expresses his gratitude to the Church
Radio, Publicity, and Mission Literature Committee
for examination of the manuscript and recommenda-
tions concerning its publication and to Dr. Sidney B.
Sperry for numerous helpful suggestions and
criticisms.

TABLE OF CONTENTS

Title page	1
Instructions to user	5
Apostasy	7
Atonement	8
Authority in the Ministry	9
Authority Necessary	9
Unauthorized Acts not Recognized by God	10
Baptism	11
Essential to Salvation	11
Performed by Immersion	11
For the Remission of Sins	12
Not Necessary for Infants	12
Book of Mormon	13
Christ's Reign on Earth	14
The Millennium	14
After the Millennium	15
Church of Jesus Christ	15
Organization	15
Members Called Saints	16
Named After Christ	17
Duties of Members	17
Faith	19
A Principle of Power	19
Stories of Faith	20
Faith and Works	21
Gathering of Israel	22
The Dispersion	22
The Gathering	22
Two Gathering Places	23
Gospel	24
The Key to Salvation	24
Preached Before the Time of Christ	25
Preached Without Charge	25
Hell	26
Between Death and the Resurrection	26
After the Resurrection	27
Hereafter	28
Holy Ghost	28
What It Is	28
Necessary for All to Receive	29
Conferred by the Laying on of Hands	29
Gifts and Functions	30
Sin Against the Holy Ghost	30
Judgment	31
Judgment at Christ's Coming	31
The Final Judgment	32
Latter Day Revelation	32
Revelation	32
The Visitation of Angels	33
Revelation Later Than the Bible Predicted	34

Man's Free Agency.. 34
Marriage.. 35
Missing Scripture.. 36
New Jerusalem.. 37
Persecution.. 38
Personality of God.. 39
    God a Personal Being.. 39
    Attributes of God.. 39
    The Holy Trinity — Three Separate Personages........................ 40
Prayer.. 41
Pre-Mortal Existence of Spirits.. 42
    Christ's Pre-Mortal Existence.. 42
    Man's Pre-Mortal Existence.. 43
    Followers of Satan Cast Out.. 43
Recreation.. 44
Repentance.. 44
    A Saving Principle.. 44
    Stories of Repentance.. 46
Restoration of the Gospel.. 47
Resurrection.. 48
    Resurrection of Christ.. 48
    Resurrection of Mankind.. 49
    Three Degrees of Glory.. 50
Sabbath Day.. 51
    Sunday, the True Sabbath.. 51
    Proper Observance of the Sabbath.. 51
Sacrament of the Lord's Supper.. 52
Salvation for the Dead.. 53
    Baptism Required of All.. 53
    Gospel Preached to the Dead by Christ.. 53
    Baptism for the Dead.. 54
Second Coming of Jesus Christ.. 54
    Christ's Coming Foretold.. 54
    Events to Precede Christ's Coming.. 56
Spiritual Gifts.. 57
    Characteristic of Christ's Church.. 57
    Healing.. 58
    Miracles Alone Not Proof of True Church...................................... 58
Tithes and Offerings.. 59
Transgression and the Fall.. 60
Urim and Thummim.. 61
Word of Wisdom.. 61
Appendix.. 63

TO THE USER

1. Symbols occasionally found after Bible citations (* † ‡ § ||) refer the user to corresponding symbols under the "Latter-day Scripture" section of the subject. In each case the latter-day scripture text sheds additional light on the Bible reference similarly checked, and the two profitably may be considered together.

2. Wherever a passage of scripture is laid in an interesting contextual setting, a consideration of which might serve to enrich the explanation and use of the reference, the fact is indicated on the index line in parentheses as "(Story setting)" or "(Story)."

3. Index words, although in some instances directly quoted parts of passages cited, usually are printed without quotation marks.

4. Books of the Bible follow the usual abbreviations. Books of the Book of Mormon are not contracted. "D & C" indicates Doctrine and Covenants. "P of GP" designates Pearl of Great Price.

5. Two blank lines added at the end of each topic and sub-topic are for the convenience of the user who may wish to add additional references of his own choosing.

COMBINATION REFERENCE

APOSTASY

Objective: To establish the necessity for a restoration of the Church of Jesus
Christ by showing that mankind turned away from the gospel anciently and
for centuries has been groping in spiritual darkness.

Bible: **Bible**

Because the everlasting covenant (of Christ; com-
pare Heb. 13:20) broken, earth to be burned........Isa. 24:1-6*..............

To world in apostasy a "marvelous work" to come........Isa. 29:13-14.............

Saints to be afflicted. False prophets to arise..............Matt. 24:9-12...........

Grievous wolves to enter the flock at Ephesus.............Acts 20:29-30...........

Paul marvels that the Saints "so soon removed"..........Gal. 1:6-9................

A falling away before Christ's second coming.............2 Thess. 2:1-11........

In the latter times some to depart from the faith.........1 Tim. 4:1-3.............

Men to have form of godliness, denying the power.......2 Tim. 3:1-5............

They shall turn away their ears. (Story setting).........2 Tim. 4:2-4...........

There shall be false teachers among you........................2 Pet. 2:1-3.............

The Church at Ephesus in a fallen state........................Rev. 2:1-5...............

Faith of the Saints at Laodicea lukewarm.....................Rev. 3:14-17...........

Powers of darkness to overcome the Saints....................Rev. 13:6-7..............

Latter Day Scripture: **Latter Day Scripture**

Loss of parts of Bible a cause of stumbling....................1 Nephi 13:24-29......

A state of apostasy. The restoration...............................2Nephi,Chaps. 28-29

Nephite apostasy and extinction prophesied..................Alma 45:8-14...........

Apostate Nephite race destroyed. (See Ether 4:3)........Mormon 8:1-8..........

Picture of Nephites in period of final apostasy.............Moroni Chap. 9........

They have broken mine everlasting covenant.................D&C 1:11-17*...........

They draw near to Me with lips (Story setting).............PofGP, Smith 2:19..

Related References: **Related References**

Behold, the darkness shall cover the earth.....................Isa. 60:2...................

A famine for the word. (Pos-
sibly fulfilled *before* Christ)......................................Amos 8:11-12............

2 TimoThy 1:15 – All Asia fallen
a way.

Concerning gospel dispensations before Christ, see "Preached before the Time of Christ."
GOSPEL.

Note. George Fox's *Book of the Martyrs* speaks of the martyrdom or exile of all of the
early apostolic leaders of the Christian Church. The effect of this as a factor in the apostasy
should not be overlooked. See PERSECUTION.

ATONEMENT

Objective: To show that: (a) the atonement of Christ opens the gateway
to the resurrection, giving mankind deliverance from the death brought by
Adam; (b) the atonement places within man's ultimate reach exaltation in
the presence of God, giving him an incentive and a purpose to overcome sin.

Bible:	Bible
He was wounded for our transgressions	Isa. 53:3-12
He shall save people from their sins. (Story setting)	Matt. 1:21-23
Jesus taught disciples that He must be killed	Matt. 16:21
Son came to give life as a ransom. (Story setting)	Matt. 20:28
The crucifixion and resurrection story. (Consult also Mark 14-16; Luke 22-24; John 18-21)	Matt. Chaps. 26-28
Sacrament, a symbol of atonement. (Story setting)	Luke 22:19-20
Behold, the Lamb of God. (Story setting)	John 1:29-36
For God so loved the world that He gave His Son	John 3:14-18
Jesus able to lay down life and take it up	John 10:17-18
I am the resurrection and the life. (Story setting)	John 11:25-26
I will draw all men to me. (Story setting)	John 12:32-33
Christ a Prince and a Savior. (Story setting)	Acts 5:29-32
Death through Adam. Life through Christ	Rom. 5:6-19
As in Adam all die, in Christ all made alive	1 Cor. 15:19-22
Christ the Mediator of the new testament	Heb. 9:15-22
Christ foreordained before foundation of world	1 Peter 1:18-20
Blood of Christ cleanses righteous from sin	1 John 1:5-7
Thou wast slain and hast redeemed us	Rev. 5:9-10
Lamb slain from the foundation of the world	Rev. 13:8

Latter Day Scripture:	Latter Day Scripture
Nephi foresees crucifixion. (Story setting)	1 Nephi 11:13-33
None can dwell in God's presence save through Messiah	2 Nephi 2:6-8
There must needs be a power of resurrection. (Chapter)	2 Nephi 9:3-9
He suffereth the pains of all men. (Chapter)	2 Nephi 9:21-22
Atonement applicable to those without law. (Chapter)	2 Nephi 9:25-27
Christ went to Jews *because* they would kill Him	2 Nephi 10:3-5
The atonement predicted. (Chapter.) (Story setting)	Mosiah 3:5-16
Salvation for the faithful through atonement	Mosiah 4:6-8
No resurrection possible without Christ	Mosiah 16:6-8
Atonement a great and last sacrifice	Alma 34:8-16
Fall and atonement discussed by Alma	Alma Chap. 42
Men not redeemed in sins but from sins	Helaman 5:9-11
Purpose of Christ's death. (Story setting, Ch. 13)	Helaman 14:15-18
I have suffered the will of the Father (Story setting)	3 Nephi 11:8-15
That I might be lifted up upon the cross	3 Nephi 27:13-22
Resurrection given to all by Christ's death	Mormon 9:12-13
I, God, have suffered these things for all	D&C 19:16-19
Atonement benefits believers in all ages	D&C 20:21-29
Raised in immortality unto eternal life	D&C 29:42-45

Little children redeemed through Christ..........................D&C 29:46-47..........
The gospel is "glad tidings" of atonement.....................D&C 76:40-42..........
Resurrection from dead is redemption of soul.................D&C 88:14-17..........

Related References: **Related References**

Salvation in Christ's name. (Story setting)...................Acts 4:12...................
Christ the author of eternal salvation............................Heb. 5:8-9................
Law of sacrifice a similitude of Christ...........................PofGP,Moses 5:6-8..

AUTHORITY IN THE MINISTRY
Authority Necessary

Objective: To show that: (a) divine authority alone empowers men to officiate in the sacred ordinances of the gospel. A "call" or urge to preach is not enough; (b) divine (priesthood) authority has been restored to earth in these latter days.

Bible: **Bible**

Aaron divinely called and authorized..............................Ex. 28:1&40:13-15....
Joshua called by prophecy and laying on of hands.......Num. 27:18-23.........
Peter promised keys of kingdom. (Story setting)..........Matt. 16:19*.............
Apostles sent to teach nations. (Story setting).............Matt. 28:19-20.........
The twelve ordained by Jesus Christ...............................Mark 3:14-15.........
The seventy called and commissioned..............................Luke 10:1, 17.........
I have chosen you and ordained you...............................John 15:16...............
Matthias chosen to be an apostle. (Story setting)........Acts 1:21-26..........
Christ visits (but does not ordain) Paul...........................Acts 9:1-6..............
Paul commissioned by laying on of hands.
   (It is possible that he had previously
   been ordained and that this was
   solely a missionary appointment.).......................Acts 13:1-3...........
Elders ordained by Paul. (Story setting).......................Acts 14:23..............
How shall they preach except (divinely) sent.................Rom. 10:14-15..........
With the laying on hands of the presbytery (elders)......1 Tim. 4:14..............
The gift that is in thee by the putting on of my hands....2 Tim. 1:6.................
Titus instructed to ordain elders in every city..............Titus 1:5.................
No man taketh this honor unto himself..........................Heb. 5:4..................
Jesus a high priest after order of Melchizedek..............Heb. 5:6, 10.............
Priesthood changed with coming of Christ. (The
   higher or Melchizedek priesthood added.).............Heb. 7:11-12............
Ye are a chosen generation, a royal priesthood.............1 Pet. 2:9.................

Latter Day Scripture: **Latter Day Scripture**

The manner after which they were ordained.................Alma 13:1-19............
Authority to baptize given Nephite disciples.
   (Story setting.) Compare 3 Nephi 12:1.................3 Nephi 11:21-22......
Authority to confer Holy Ghost bestowed on disciples....3 Nephi 18:36-37......
Manner of ordaining priests and teachers.....................Moroni 3:1-4.............
Joseph Smith waited long for authority; "not yet or-
   dained" 9 years after visit of Father and Son...D&C 5:17...............

Aaronic priesthood conferred by John the Baptist..........D&C 13.....................
Apostleship conferred by Peter, James, and John..........D&C 27:12-13..........
None to preach except properly ordained.....................D&C 42:11.............
Descent of Melchizedek priesthood, Adam to Moses......D&C 84:6-17..............
Descent of Aaronic priesthood, Aaron to John.............D&C 84:18-28..........
Revelation on priesthood. Duties of various officers......D&C 107.................
Priesthood operative only in righteousness.....................D&C 121:34-36.......
Priesthood keys held by only one on earth at a time........D&C 132:7...............
Power to seal restored through the priesthood..............D&C 132:45-46*.......
Aaronic priesthood restored...PGP,Smith 2:68-73..

Related References: Related References

For further concerning officers in the Church, see "Organization," CHURCH OF JESUS CHRIST.

Unauthorized Acts Not Recognized by God

Objective: To show that the sacred ordinances of the gospel performed by men *without* divine authority are not acceptable to God.

Bible: Bible

Saul rebuked for sacrifice. (Story setting)....................1 Sam. 13:8-14..........
Uzza smitten for touching the ark. (Story setting)........1 Chron. 13:9-10......
King Uzziah enters temple. (Story setting)..................2 Chron 26:16-21....
I have not sent these prophets, yet they ran..................Jer. 23:21.................
Many will say, "Have we not prophesied"....................Matt. 7:21-29............
Paul rebaptizes converts of unauthorized teacher..........Acts 19:1-6..............
Jesus I know and Paul I know: but who are ye?...........Acts 19:13-16...........

Latter Day Scripture: Latter Day Scripture

None in the land had authority. (Story setting)...........Mosiah 21:33............
Baptisms performed without authority are of no value..D&C 22:1-4.............
None to preach except they be properly ordained.........D&C 42:11...............

Related References: Related References

See also "Miracles Alone Not Proof of True Church." SPIRITUAL GIFTS.

BAPTISM
Essential to Salvation

Objective: To show that baptism is a necessary requirement for entrance into the kingdom of heaven.

Bible: Bible

John the Baptist baptized, preparing the way...............Matt. 3:1-12..............
Jesus was baptized to fulfill all righteousness.................Matt. 3:13-17...........
Apostles sent to baptize nations. (Story setting)..........Matt. 28:19-20.........

He that believeth and is baptized shall be saved............Mark 16:15-16..........
Refusing baptism called rejecting counsel of God..........Luke 7:28-30..............
Except a man be born of water. (Story setting)............John 3:5..............
Repent and be baptized. (Story setting).....................Acts 2:37-38..............
Cornelius was baptized. (Story setting) (Note v. 6.)....Acts 10:47-48..........
Paul baptized prison keeper. (Story setting)................Acts 16:25-33..........
Paul was baptized. (Story setting) (Comp. Acts 9:6.)....Acts 22:10-16............
Baptism the appointed way to "put on Christ".............Gal. 3:27..............
Baptisms (of water and Spirit) fundamental..................Heb. 6:1-2................
Even baptism doth also now save us...............................1 Pet. 3:21..............

Latter Day Scripture: **Latter Day Scripture**

All must be baptized or receive condemnation................2 Nephi 9:23-24........
Christ's baptism a binding example on all.......................2 Nephi 31:5-9..........
Baptism the gateway. "Wherefore do the things"........2 Nephi 31:17..........
Baptism taught by Savior. (Story setting)....................3 Nephi 11:33-34......
Men to repent and be baptized. (Story setting)............3 Nephi 27:16-20......
Go forth baptizing with water, preparing the way.........D&C 39:19-24..........
Those who refuse baptism condemned..........................D&C 84:74..............
Law revealed in the beginning. Adam baptized...........PGP,Moses 6:51-68..
Baptism taught by Enoch. (Story setting)...................PGP,Moses 7:10-11..
Baptism taught by Noah. (Story setting)....................PGP,Moses 8:23-24..

Related References: **Related References**

None in the land able to baptize. (Story setting)..........Mosiah 21:33............
Conditions of baptism among Nephites.......................Moroni 6:1-4..............
Conditions of baptism for Church today......................D&C 20:37..............
Baptisms performed without authority are of no value....D&C 22:1-4..............

Performed by Immersion

Objective: To show that New Testament scripture supports the testimony of latter day revelation that baptism is performed by complete immersion in water.

Bible: **Bible**

John baptized in river Jordan. (Story setting)..............Matt. 3:5-6................
Jesus went up out of the water. (Story setting)............Matt. 3:16................
John baptized in Ænon because much water there.......John 3:23............
They went down into the water. (Story setting)..........Acts 8:38-39..............
Baptism likened to burial and planting.........................Rom. 6:3-5..............
Buried with Him in baptism...Col. 2:12..............

Latter Day Scripture: **Latter Day Scripture**

Alma baptizes in waters of Mormon. (Story setting)......Mosiah 18:8-17..........
Christ explains form of baptism. (Story setting).........3 Nephi 11:22-26......
Nephi was baptized by immersion. (Story setting)......3 Nephi 19:10-12......
Form of baptism and words of ceremony given.............D&C 20:72-74...........
Immersion required for celestial glory............................D&C 76:50-53.........
Authority to baptize restored......................................PGP,Smith 2:68-73..

Related References: Related References
   Strait is the gate, and narrow is the way..........................Matt. 7:13-14............
   One Lord, one faith, one baptism......................................Eph. 4:5...................

For the Remission of Sins

Objective: To show that the repentant sinner, on compliance with the ordinance of baptism, obtains forgiveness of sin.

Bible: Bible
   John preached baptism for the remission of sins............Mark 1:4...................
   Baptism of repentance for remission of sins...................Luke 3:3....................
   For the remission of sins. (Story setting)......................Acts 2:38.................
   Wash away thy sins. (Story setting).............................Acts 22:16...............

Latter Day Scripture: Latter Day Scripture
   Be baptized that ye may be washed from sin.................Alma 7:14.................
   A remission of their sins. (Story setting, Ch. 11)..........3 Nephi 12:2.............
   Fulfilling commandments brings remission.....................Moroni 8:25-26.........
   Baptism for remission of sins. (Story setting)...............PofGP, Smith 2:69..

Related References: Related References
Other   { Baptism the way to enter the Church......Acts 2:41....................
purposes   { The appointed way to "put on Christ"......Gal. 3:27...................
of baptism   { A covenant with God. (Story setting)......Mosiah 18:8-17.........

Not Necessary for Infants

Objective: To show that baptism is not required of infant children who are too young to know right from wrong.

Bible: Bible
   Jesus blessed, but did not baptize, little children............Mark 10:13-16.........
   Candidates must be capable of believing.........................Mark 16:16...............
   Philip baptizes "men and women." (Story setting).....Acts 8:12...................
   Must be able to work righteousness. (Story setting)......Acts 10:34-35...........
   Mankind judged according to works.
      (Reasonably, infants, incapable of
      wrongdoing, will not be condemned.)......................Rev. 20:12.................

Latter Day Scripture: Latter Day Scripture
   Baptism of infants wrong, Mormon explains...................Moroni 8:4-22............
   Age of accountability necessary for membership............D&C 20:71.................
   Satan not allowed to tempt little children......................D&C 29:46-48...........
   Children to be baptized when eight years old.................D&C 68:25-27...........

Related References: **Related References**

Childhood humility necessary. (Story setting).............Matt. 18:3.................

Note. The baptism of Stephanas' household is sometimes urged as a point favoring infant baptism. (1 Cor. 1:16.) That the family was mature, however, may be inferred from 1 Cor. 16:15-16.
Baptism for the Dead. See SALVATION FOR THE DEAD.

BOOK OF MORMON

Objective: To show that the Book of Mormon is a scriptural record of God's dealings with a branch of the house of Israel that inhabited America anciently and that it contains the fullness of the everlasting gospel as delivered by the Savior to them.

Bible: Bible

People spread over *all* earth at fall of Babel...................Gen. 11:1-9*.............
Joseph's branches to run over wall. (Nephite crossing of ocean wall, a plausible fulfillment.)........Gen. 49:22-26............
Truth shall spring out of the earth. (Unearthing of Book of Mormon possibly indicated.)............Psalm 85:10-11..........
A people, "unto Me [the Lord] as Ariel [Jerusalem]" to speak out of the ground...................Isa. 29:2-4.................
Vision of all as words of a book that is sealed...............Isa. 29:11-14†............
Stick of Judah (Bible) and Joseph to be joined...........Ezek. 37:16-21‡.........
Parable of three measures of meal. (Vague, though possible, allusion to branches of Israel.)........Luke 13:20-21............
"Other sheep I have." (Compare Matt. 15:24).............John 10:15-16§.........

Latter Day Scripture   Latter Day Scripture

What the Book of Mormon is..Forepart of B. of M.
Testimony of three witnesses and eight...........................Forepart of B. of M.
Nephite records, history of Joseph's seed......................1 Nephi 5:14-16‡......
Latter day scriptures, a witness for the Bible.................1 Nephi 13:38-40......
Seer predicted. B. of M. and Bible to be as one...........2 Nephi 3:6-15..........
Three witnesses and a sealed book foretold.....................2 Nephi 27:6-26........
Many shall say, "A Bible! A Bible"...........................2 Nephi 29:3-14........
Ye are they of whom I said, "Other sheep I have"........3 Nephi 15:21-24§....
B. of M. given to try men's faith. More to come.........3 Nephi 26:8-11........
Moroni ends Book of Mormon; tells destiny.................Mormon Chap. 8......
Jaredites come to America from Tower of Babel...........Ether 1:33*...............
Book of Mormon given to show world way of escape. America a choice land. (Story setting)........Ether 2:9-12..............
How truth of Book of Mormon may be known. (Chapter)....................................Moroni 10:2-5..........
Moroni testifies mightily to the truth of his writings....Moroni 10:27-29........
Prayer of ancients that record be kept for us.................D&C 10:45-52..........
Story of Book of Mormon origin..PGP,Smith 2:28-75..
The learned man and the "sealed book".........................PGP,Smith 2:63-65..

Related References:	Related References
As with Book of Mormon, so with resurrection of Savior, the message given to world by witnesses......Acts 10:40-42............	
By witnesses shall every word be established..................2 Cor. 13:1................	
American Indians of Israel. Dark skin explained.........2 Nephi 5:21-25.........	
Lord gives line upon line, precept upon precept.............2 Nephi 28:29-30......	
Visions of Jared's brother sealed with plates...................Ether 4:4-8...............	
Picture of Nephites at time of downfall...........................Moroni Chap. 9........	

NOTE: Of special interest to Christ-professing people is the account of Jesus' visit to the Nephite nation, which event is not only the greatest episode of the history of Ancient America but also the literary climax of the Book of Mormon. For a conversation, or short sermon, excerpts from 3 Nephi, Chaps. 8-11, 15, and 17 are suggested.

For further concerning the necessity of latter-day scripture, see MISSING SCRIPTURE.

CHRIST'S REIGN ON EARTH

The Millennium

Objective: To show that Christ's coming will usher in the Millennial reign, an era of a thousand years of righteousness and peace.

Bible:	Bible
The wolf also shall dwell with the lamb..........................Isa. 11:1-9................	
Strangers shall feed flocks. Ye shall be priests.............Isa. 61:4-6................	
There shall be no more thence an infant of days...........Isa. 65:17-25.............	
The land to become like the garden of Eden...................Ezek. 36:34-38..........	
Israel to be one nation under a king named David.......Ezek. 37:21-28..........	
The kingdom to be given to Saints of most High...........Dan. 7:27...................	
The Lord shall roar out of Zion and Jerusalem.............Joel 3:15-17...............	
Hills to melt, waste cities to be inhabited......................Amos 9:13-15............	
They shall beat their swords into plowshares.................Mic. 4:1-7................	
Lord to be king over earth. (Story setting)...................Zech. 14:4-9..............	
Kingdoms of world to be Lord's. (Story setting).........Rev. 11:15................	
Satan to be bound a thousand years..............................Rev. 20:1-6...............	

Latter Day Scripture:	Latter Day Scripture
Holy One to reign. Righteousness to bind Satan..........1 Nephi 22:24-26......	
Satan to have no power for "a long time"........................2 Nephi 30:10-18......	
Christ to dwell with men on earth..................................D&C 29:9-11.............	
In Millennium resurrection to be quick change..............D&C 63:49-53.............	
A new song. Millennial era heralded..............................D&C 84:96-102..........	
The 12 vineyards. Earth to be visited in its turn..........D&C 88:51-62............	
Satan shall not be loosed for a thousand years.................D&C 88:110.............	
Glorious description of Millennial age given..................D&C 101:22-31.........	
Ocean to be driven back and continents made one........D&C 133:17-25.........	
City of Enoch to return. The thousand years................PGP, Moses 7:60-66	

Related References: **Related References**

    Wicked not to live till thousand years ended.................D&C 88:100-102......

See also SECOND COMING OF JESUS CHRIST.

After the Millennium

Objective: To show that at the close of the Millennium Satan will be loosed for a little season, after which the earth will be crowned with celestial glory and become the home of the righteous in eternity.

Bible: **Bible**

    Then cometh the end. Death done away........................1 Cor. 15:23-28..........
    When the thousand years are ended Satan loosed..........Rev. 20:7-15*............
    And I saw a new heaven and a new earth....................Rev. 21:1-4...............

Latter Day Scripture: **Latter Day Scripture**

    There shall be a new heaven and a new earth.............D&C 29:22-28..........
    Satan to be loosed for a little season...........................D&C 43:30-33..........
    Sanctified earth to be as sea of glass...........................D&C 77:1.................
    Earth to be sanctified and celestialized.........................D&C 88:17-20..........
    Celestialized earth to be home of the righteous.............D&C 88:25-26..........
    Satan loosed. The earth's final war.............................D&C 88:111-115*....
    Sanctified earth to be as Urim and Thummim...............D&C 130:8-11..........

Related References: **Related References**

    Jesus promised meek to inherit the earth.......................Matt 5:5...................

CHURCH OF JESUS CHRIST

Organization

Objective: To show — in evidence of a restoration of the gospel — that the Church of Jesus Christ of Latter-day Saints possesses essentially the same scheme of organization that identified Christ's Church anciently.

Bible: **Bible**

    Apostles chosen. (Their ordination, Mark 3:14)............Luke 6:12-16..............
    Seventies chosen to go forth to preach............................Luke 10:1.................
    Quorum of Twelve continued. (Story setting)..............Acts 1:21-26..............
    Prophets and teachers in the church at Antioch...........Acts 13:1.................
    Elders ordained by Paul. (Story setting).......................Acts 14:23.................
    Philip, the evangelist. (Story setting).............................Acts 21:8...................
    A certain prophet named Agabus. (Story setting)........Acts 21:9-11..............

Apostles, prophets, teachers. "And God hath set"........1 Cor. 12:27-31.........
Paul also an apostle by Jesus Christ................................Gal. 1:1....................
Built upon foundation of apostles and prophets............Eph. 2:19-21..............
"And he gave some." Purpose of officers, v. 12.
    How long needed, 13. Results when lacking, 14.....Eph. 4:11-14..............
Bishops and deacons at Philippi.................................Philip. 1:1..................
The office and qualifications of a bishop.........................1 Tim. 3:1-7.............
The office and qualifications of a deacon........................1 Tim. 3:8-10...........
Do the work of an evangelist. (Story setting)..............2 Tim. 4:5................
Titus instructed to ordain elders in every city...............Titus 1:5.................
Jesus, a high priest after the order of Melchizedek.......Heb. 5:6, 10...........
Is any sick among you? Let him call for elders............James 5:14...............
The elders which are among you....................................1 Pet. 5:1................

Latter Day Scripture: **Latter Day Scripture**

Seer, revelator, prophet defined. (Story setting)............Mosiah 8:13-18.........
Savior chooses Nephite Twelve. (Story setting)............3 Nephi
                                           11:21-22 & 12:1........
Order of Twelve continued; later ordinations...............4 Nephi 1:14..............
Concerning ordination of priests and teachers..............Moroni 3:1-4.............
Duties of elders, priests, teachers, deacons.....................D&C 20:38-60............
Church courts for the settlement of disputes.................D&C 102:24-32........
Revelation on priesthood. Duties of various officers....D&C 107...................
Purpose of offices; how and when filled.......................D&C 124:143-144....

Related References: **Related References**

Seventy elders in Moses' day. (Story setting)..............Num. 11:16-25.........
Church established by Jesus; not the scheme of.........⎰Matt. 16:15-18.........
    later organizers. (See also passages above)...........⎱Matt. 18:15-17.........
High priest. (Here, a priest under *Mosaic* order)........Heb. 5:1....................
Priesthood changed with coming of Christ. (The
    higher or Melchizedek priesthood added)...........Heb. 7:11-12..............

Concerning the objection that John the Baptist was the last prophet God intended to send mankind, see Note 1 following "Revelation Later Than the Bible Predicted." LATTER DAY REVELATION.

For further concerning priesthood in the Church, see "Authority Necessary." AUTHORITY IN THE MINISTRY.

Members Called Saints

Objective: To show that one of the identifying features of Christ's church is that its members are called Saints.

Bible: **Bible**

To all in Rome called to be Saints...................................Rom. 1:7....................
A contribution for the Saints at Jerusalem.....................Rom. 15:26...............
As in all churches of the Saints......................................1 Cor. 14:33..............
For the perfecting of the Saints......................................Eph. 4:12..................
To all the Saints in Christ Jesus....................................Philip. 1:1.................
Salute every Saint in Christ Jesus.................................Philip. 4:21-22.........

To the Saints and faithful brethren in Christ..................Col. 1:2.....................
A people to be called Saints at Christ's coming.............2 Thess. 1:7-10..........

Latter Day Scripture: **Latter Day Scripture**

Nephi sees latter day Church, "Saints of God"..............1 Nephi 14:12...........
Church of Jesus Christ of Latter-day Saints....................D&C 115:4....... ....

Related References: **Related References**

_____

_____

Named After Christ

Objective: To show that one of the identifying features of Christ's church
is that it bears His name.

Bible   **Bible**

None other name given. (Story setting)........................Acts 4:12...................
As husband head of wife, Christ head of Church. (In-
  ference is Church should receive Christ's name)....Eph. 5:23.................

Latter Day Scripture: **Latter Day Scripture**

How be it My Church save it be called in My name?......3 Nephi 27:1-8.........
Church of Jesus Christ of Latter-day Saints....................D&C 115:4...............

Related References: **Related References**

Be ye therefore perfect, even as your Father..................Matt. 5:48.................

_____

_____

DUTIES OF MEMBERS

Objective: To show that membership in Christ's Church is the beginning,
not the end, of salvation. After baptism constant faith, repentance, and
good works are necessary to lead men finally to perfection.

Bible: **Bible**

To fear God and keep commandments is duty of man....Eccl. 12:13...............
Be ye therefore perfect, even as your Father..................Matt. 5:48.................
Sermon on the Mount. (For members and others)........Matt. Chaps. 5-7......
Ten Commandments restated
  by Christ. (Comp. Ex. 20)..Matt. 19:16-22...........
Unto whomsoever much is given is much required........Luke 12:47-48...........
Paul's discourse to the Saints on charity (love).............1 Cor. Chap. 13........
Works of the flesh and of the Spirit told....................Gal. 5:13-26.............
"Wherefore putting away lying." Counsel for all........Eph. 4:25-32.............
Awake thou that sleepest. (Entire chapter).................Eph. 5:14-20.............
Advice to children, parents. The armor of God...........Eph. 6:1-18...............

Rejoice always. Think on whatsoever
true, honest, or of good report..............................Philip. 4:4-8..............
Be not deceived by philosophies of men..........................Col. 2:6:8.....................
Counsel for husbands, wives, children, servants.............Col. 3:12-25..............
Respect leaders. Avoid appearance of evil.....................1 Thess. 5:12-22........
After baptism, "Let us go on unto perfection"...............Heb. 6:1-3.................
Pure religion is to visit fatherless and widows.............James 1:26-27...........
Add to your faith virtue; and to virtue knowledge........2 Pet. 1:5-8................

Latter Day Scripture: **Latter Day Scripture**

Live righteously. Prepare for the judgment.................2 Nephi 9:27; 39-52..
Baptism is only a gateway to the path..........................2 Nephi 31:17-20.....
Humility and charity. The teaching of children..........Mosiah 4:11-30..........
Be submissive and gentle, easy to be entreated.............Alma 7:23-24...........
Fear not little flock; do good. Look unto Me.............D&C 6:32-37...........
Repent; worship Father. Man may fall from grace......D&C 20:29-34..........
Put on the whole armor of God................................D&C 27:15-18..........
Let every man esteem his brother as himself.................D&C 38:23-30..........
Go out from the wicked. Warn neighbor.....................D&C 38:40-42..........
Grow in grace and in knowledge of the truth.................D&C 50:40-46..........
Let no man break the laws of the land..........................D&C 58:21-22..........
Men should be anxiously engaged in a good cause..........D&C 58:26-29..........
Go to the house of prayer on the Sabbath day...............D&C 59:9-13.............
Be of good cheer. Be watchful. Pray always...............D&C 61:36-39..........
Of you it is required to forgive all men.........................D&C 64:8-14.............
Be not weary. A great work being founded...................D&C 64:33-34..........
Parents to teach children gospel principles....................D&C 68:25-31..........
Necessary to overcome all things for celestial glory........D&C 76:50-53, 60...
Greater revelations bring responsibilities.......................D&C 82:2-4............
Draw near unto Me. Cast away idle thoughts.............D&C 88:63-69..........
Teach one another. Read best books. Be not idle.......D&C 88:118-126......
Correct children. Men failing in this chastized.............D&C 93:39-49..........
Members called to be the savor of men.........................D&C 101:39-40.......
Let every man learn his duty and act in office...............D&C 107:99-100.......
Use priesthood in the spirit of love, not force.................D&C 121:34-46........

Related References: **Related References**

To obey is better than sacrifice. (Story setting)............1 Sam. 15:23.............
Respect for authority. Story of David and Saul............1 Sam. Chaps. 24, 26
Parable of ten virgins. "Then shall the kingdom".......Matt. 25:1-13...........
For I was an hungered, and ye gave Me meat...............Matt. 25:31-46.........
The faithful to know mysteries of God.........................Alma 26:22...............
He that continueth in light receiveth light.....................D&C 50:24...............
The obedient to know mysteries of the kingdom...........D&C 63:23................
All mysteries to be revealed to righteous......................D&C 76:5-10............
Blessings ahead not yet understood...............................D&C 78:17-18..........
I, the Lord, am bound when ye do what I say...............D&C 82:10................
All blessings are predicated upon law............................D&C 130:20-21........

For related subjects, see FAITH AND WORKS (embracing OBEDIENCE), PRAYER,
REPENTANCE, TITHES AND OFFERINGS, WORD OF WISDOM.

FAITH

A Principle of Power

Objective: To show that faith is the first principle of the gospel and a universal law of progress necessary to man's salvation.

Bible: · **Bible**

Trust in God. "Behold the fowls of the air"	Matt. 6:26-30
Faith will move mountains. (Story setting)	Matt. 17:20
All things possible to believers. (Story setting)	Mark 9:23
Belief basis of eternal life. "For God so loved"	John 3:16-18
The just shall live by faith	Rom. 1:16-17
Faith comes by hearing the word of God	Rom. 10:17
We walk by faith not by sight	2 Cor. 5:7
Baptism, laying on of hands, repentance, faith	Heb. 6:1-2
Faith is substance (assurance) of things hoped for	Heb. Chap. 11
If any lack wisdom let him ask God in faith	James 1:5-6
The prayer of faith to save the sick	James 5:14-15
Fervent prayer availeth much. Elias' power	James 5:16-18
Salvation of souls is the end of faith	1 Pet. 1:9

Latter Day Scripture: · **Latter Day Scripture**

A hope for things which are true. (Story setting)	Alma 32:21
How faith is developed. Chapter. (Story setting)	Alma 32:26-43
B. of M. given to test men's faith. More to come	3 Nephi 26:8-10
Great things to be shown those who have faith	Ether 4:7-19
Moroni discusses the power of faith	Ether 12:6-22
Mount Zerin moved through faith	Ether 12:29-31
Faith saves. Miracles wrought by its power	Moroni 7:21-39
By faith truth of Book of Mormon may be known	Moroni 10:4
Miracles of healing possible through faith	D&C 35:9-11
Faith and the power to be healed	D&C 42:48-52
Faith comes not by signs but signs by faith	D&C 63:8-11
Signs that follow belief enumerated	D&C 84:65-72

Related References: · **Related References**

Faith to the end needed. "He that shall endure"	Matt. 24:13
Salvation in Christ's name. (Faith should be in Him)	Acts 4:12

NOTE: The supposition that it matters not what a man believes so long as he is sincere in his convictions seemingly lacks valid scriptural support. Religious belief must be based upon truth to be acceptable to God. Consider Matt. 15:8-9; Matt. 27:25; John 16:2-3; Acts 26:9-11; Rom. 10:1-3.

Stories of Faith

Objective: To show, by illustration, that faith is a principle of power and a universal law of progress necessary to man's salvation.

Bible:	Bible
Abraham's test. The command to sacrifice Isaac	Gen. 22:1-14
Stand still and see the salvation of the Lord	Ex. Chap. 14
David's great faith. The slaying of Goliath	1 Sam. Chap. 17
Job's trial of faith. The affliction of boils	Job Chaps. 1-2, 42
Faith of Hebrew youths. The fiery furnace	Dan. Chap. 3
The Centurion's great faith. Servant healed	Matt. 8:5-13
Jesus walks on water. Peter tries and falters	Matt. 14:22-33
Gentile woman's daughter healed through faith	Matt. 15:21-28
Savior heals lunatic. Faith moves mountains	Matt. 17:14-20
Jesus causes tree to wither. Faith discussed	Matt. 21:17-22
Jesus stills the tempest. "Peace be still"	Mark 4:36-40
Jesus unable to do mighty works due to unbelief	Mark 6:1-6
Woman touches Jesus and is healed through faith	Luke 8:43-48
Jesus raises ruler's daughter. "Believe only"	Luke 8:49-56
Blind man healed. Amazing unbelief of Jews	John Chap. 9
Jesus raises Lazarus from the dead	John 11:1-46
Peter and John heal crippled beggar	Acts 3:1-10
Peter's prayer of faith raises woman from dead	Acts 9:36-42

Latter Day Scripture:	Latter Day Scripture
Nephi's faith. The plates of Laban obtained	1 Nephi Chaps. 3-4
Nephi bound with cords. Delivered by faith	1 Nephi 7:16-21
The Liahona found. Operative through faith	1 Ne. 16:9-10, 26-29
Nephi withstands assailants by faith. (Chapter)	1 Nephi 17:45-55
The prayer in the woods. Enos' faith	Enos 1:1-19
Lord heeds faith and prayers of captive Nephites	Mosiah 24:8-25
Angel visits Alma. (Due to father's faith, v. 14)	Mosiah 27:8-37
A prison falls. Alma's mighty faith	Alma Chap. 14
Zeezrom healed according to his faith	Alma 15:1-12
Faithful Lamanites bow before enemies	Alma Chap. 24
Helaman's 2,000 young men preserved by faith	Alma Chaps. 56-58
The great faith of two brothers. The circle of fire	Helaman 5:14-52
Nephi's power of faith. Raises brother to life	3 Nephi 7:15-20
Through faith brother of Jared sees the Lord	Ether Chap. 3
Satan obeys Moses' command of faith	PGP, Moses 1:12-25
Enoch's faith causes enemies to flee	PGP, Moses 7:13-16
Visit of Father and Son follows prayer of faith	PGP, Smith 2:11-19
Angel Moroni comes after prayer of faith	PGP, Smith 2:29-32

Related References:

FAITH AND WORKS

Objective: To show that obedience to the requirements of the gospel and active righteous living are necessary qualities of the faith that saves.

Bible: Bible

Those who do God's will given kingdom............................Matt. 7:21-23............
Doers of the word build their house upon a rock............Matt. 7:24-27............
Son to come and reward all according to their works....Matt. 16:27..............
Doers to inherit kingdom. "I was an hungered"............Matt. 25:31-46.........
Baptism a required work. "Go ye into all"....................Mark 16:15-16.........
Why call Me "Lord, Lord" and do not things I say......Luke 6:46-49............
The Samaritan's example of good works.........................Luke 10:25-37...........
"If any man will do His will." (Story setting)..............John 7:16-17............
If ye continue in My word then are ye disciples...........John 8:31-32...........
If ye love Me keep My commandments.........................John 14:15..............
Works of repentance and baptism. (Story setting)......Acts 2:37-38............
Workers of good accepted. (Story setting)...................Acts 10:34-35...........
Lord to render to all according to their deeds...............Rom. 2:6-8...............
Not hearers but doers of the law to be justified............Rom. 2:13.................
Vengeance to fall on those who obey not gospel............2 Thess. 1:7-10.........
Eternal salvation to all that obey..................................Heb. 5:8-9................
Be ye doers of the word and not hearers only..............James 1:22-25..........
Pure religion is to visit fatherless and widows..............James 1:26-27..........
Faith without works is dead. Devils believe................James 2:14-26..........
To know good and to do it not is sin..........................James 4:17...............
We know Him if we keep His commandments...............1 John 2:3-5............
"And I saw the dead." All judged by works................Rev. 20:12...............
Blessed are they that do His commandments................Rev. 22:14...............

Latter Day Scripture: Latter Day Scripture

Men to be judged according to their works....................1 Nephi 15:30-33......
Baptism a beginning. Other works needed after............2 Nephi 31:17-20......
Salvation comes to the diligent. Humility needed.......Mosiah 4:6-16...........
Alma tells qualities that produce good works................Alma 7:23-24...........
All shall reap the reward of their works........................Alma 9:27-28...........
I, the Lord, am bound when ye do what I say...............D&C 82:10.............
All blessings predicated on obedience to law..................D&C 130:20-21........

Related References: Related References

To obey is better than sacrifice. (Story setting)...........1 Sam. 15:22.............
By obedience Naaman healed in Jordan........................2 Kings 5:1-14.........
False prophets known by their fruits............................Matt. 7:15-20...........
He that shall endure to the end to be saved..................Matt. 24:13..............

the fact, however, that though God's gift of salvation is extended to all, only those who will receive it by obeying the principles that make it attainable do, in fact, receive it. "God's grace lowers the ladder, but man must do the climbing."

Note 2. Romans 10:9 has been interpreted by some to mean that confession and belief are the sole requisites of salvation. It should be observed, however, that Paul was addressing a group of people who were already members of the Church (Rom. 1:7-8) and that the quality of belief about which he spoke was that which leads to righteousness (Rom. 10:10). (Note also verses 11-17.)

Concerning works required after baptism, see DUTIES OF MEMBERS.

FALL OF ADAM
See TRANSGRESSION AND THE FALL

GATHERING OF ISRAEL
The Dispersion

Objective: To introduce the subject of "The Gathering" by showing, first, how Israel was scattered anciently.

Bible:	Bible
The Lord warns Israel of eventual scattering	Deut. 4:25-28
Israel again warned of dispersion	Deut. 28:25, 37, 64
Northern Kingdom of Israel (10 tribes) taken captive. Entire chapter. ("A considerable population must have been left behind." Dummelow)	2 Kings 17:18-23
First dispersion of Southern Kingdom of Judah	2 Chron. 36:11-20*
Final scattering of Jews predicted by Christ	Luke 21:20-24
The twelve tribes scattered abroad	James 1:1

Latter Day Scripture:	Latter Day Scripture
Lehi foresees Judah's captivity and leaves Jerusalem	1 Nephi Chaps. 1-2*
Nephite migration part of the prophesied dispersion	1 Nephi 10:12-14
Israel to be scattered among all nations	1 Nephi 22:3-4
Christ reveals (10) tribes still scattered	3 Nephi 16:1-5

Related References: Related References

_____

_____

The Gathering

Objective: To show that: (a) the scriptures predict a gathering of Israel in the latter days; (b) the Restored Church's role in the prophesied gathering bears witness of its divine mission and authority.

Bible:	Bible
The Lord to return Israel from all nations	Deut. 30:1-6
Gather My Saints together unto Me	Psalm 50:3-5
The Lord to recover a remnant of His people	Isa. 11:11-13

Elect to return. Desert to blossom as rose......................Isa. 35:1-10................
One of a city and two of a family to be taken................Jer. 3:14-18................
Lord liveth that brought Israel from *north*....................Jer. 16:14-15..............
Israel gathered by fishers and hunters.............................Jer. 16:16..................
I will bring them from the *north* country.......................Jer. 31:7-12................
Israel to be gathered out of the countries......................Ezek. 20:33-36..........
Gathered from the people among whom scattered..........Ezek. 28:25-26..........
Israel to be taken out from among heathen....................Ezek. 37:21-27..........
Righteous to be gathered from the four winds................Matt. 24:31................
A voice from heaven to proclaim gathering.....................Rev. 18:4-8*.............

Latter Day Scripture: **Latter Day Scripture**

Jews to believe in Christ and be restored......................2 Nephi 10:6-9..........
The scattering and gathering explained...........................2 Nephi 25:14-18......
Jews to accept gospel and gather to Jerusalem.............3 Nephi 20:29-46......
Gathering to begin with restoration of gospel................3 Nephi 21:26-29......
Saints to gather in view of coming tribulation.............D&C 29:7-8...............
Saints to gather to Zion as wars decreed abroad..........D&C 63:33-37..........
The righteous removed as wheat from the tares.............D&C 101:65-68.........
Keys given for return of Israel and 10 tribes.................D&C 110:11................
Gathering announced. Also D&C 29:7-8......................D&C 133:6-15*.........
Lost (10) tribes to return from the north.....................D&C 133:26-34..........
Elect finally to be assembled at City of Zion...............PGP, Moses 7:60-62
Gathering of elect. Gathering of remainder.................PGP, Smith 1:27-37

Related References: **Related References**

_____

_____

_____

Note 1. Latter day revelation testifies to the Ephraimite descent of most of the Saints.
The tribe of Ephraim is thus the leader in the prophesied gathering.

Note 2. Jerusalem was dedicated to the return of the Jews by Apostle Orson Hyde,
acting by official appointment in behalf of the Church, October 24, 1841.

Two Gathering Places

Objective: To show that the scriptures declare two separate centers of gathering, Jerusalem, which is again to be established, and Zion, which is to be
built.

Bible.   **Bible**

Out of Zion to go law; word of the Lord, Jerusalem........Isa. 2:2-3.....................
Concerning the inhabitants of Zion and Jerusalem........Isa. 4:2-4....................
The holy *cities*, Zion and Jerusalem.............................Isa. 64:10....................
It shall be said to Jerusalem and to Zion.......................Zeph. 3:14-16.............
The *cities*, Zion and Jerusalem....................................Zech. 1:16-17.............

Latter Day Scripture: **Latter Day Scripture**

Israel to gather to New Jerusalem and old....................3 Nephi 20:22, 29......
New Jerusalem to be center of gathering.......................3 Nephi 21:20-25......
Gathering to separate centers explained.......................Ether 13:4-11............

Israel to gather to Zion and Jerusalem..........................D&C 133:6-15..........
Elect to gather to New Jerusalem, called Zion...............PGP, Moses 7:60-62

Related References: Related References

_____

Note. Dr. Talmage observes that Jerusalem is sometimes called Zion in scripture, "owing to the fact that a certain hill within the Jerusalem of old was known specifically as Zion, or Mount Zion." James E. Talmage, *Articles of Faith*, p. 345. In stricter usage, as in the above, the terms designate two distinct and separate city capitals.
For references bearing more fully on the New Jerusalem, or Zion, see NEW JERUSALEM

GOD

See PERSONALITY OF GOD

GOSPEL

The Key to Salvation

Objective: To show that the gospel of Jesus Christ is an unchangeable plan for man's salvation by which mankind will be judged and that a knowledge of its divinity and saving power may be obtained by all who earnestly seek after it.

Bible: Bible

He that believes gospel and is baptized to be saved.......Mark 16:15-16..........
He shall know of the doctrine. (Story setting)..............John 7:16-17..............
Ye shall know truth and truth shall make you free.......John 8:31-32..............
The word spoken by Christ to judge men.......................John 12:48................
Salvation in Christ's name. (Story setting)...................Acts 4:12..................
The gospel is the power of God unto salvation...............Rom. 1:16-17............
Mankind to be judged according to the gospel.............Rom. 2:16................
One gospel; preachers of any other condemned.............Gal. 1:6-9................
One Lord, one faith, one baptism...................................Eph. 4:5.....................
Vengeance to fall on those who obey not gospel.............2 Thess. 1:7-10..........
Eternal salvation to all that obey....................................Heb. 5:8-9................
Christ the same yesterday, today, and forever.............Heb. 13:8................
The gospel called the perfect law of liberty...................James 1:25................

Latter Day Scripture: Latter Day Scripture

Vision of the rod of iron. (Comp. 1 Nephi 15:21-36)......1 Nephi Chap. 8......
And this is the gospel. (Story setting)..........................3 Nephi 27:13-22......
By the power of Holy Ghost truth may be known.......Moroni 10:4-5...........
Verily, I say unto you, this is my gospel.......................D&C 33:10-12............
The gospel is "glad tidings" of atonement....................D&C 76:40-42.........
The gospel is the "everlasting covenant".......................D&C 133:57.............

Related References: Related References

_____

Preached Before the Time of Christ

Objective: To show the plausibility of the claim that Mormonism represents a restoration of the gospel in our age by showing that there have been gospel dispensations before.

Bible: **Bible**

Israelites drank of the Rock which was Christ.................1 Cor. 10:1-4.............
The gospel was preached before unto Abraham.............Gal. 3:8....................
To us gospel preached as well as unto them...................Heb. 4:2....................

Latter Day Scripture: **Latter Day Scripture**

The dispensation of the gospel of Abraham...................D&C 110:12.............
The gospel was preached from the beginning.................PGP, Moses 5:58-59
The gospel law was revealed to Adam...........................PGP, Moses 6:51-68
The gospel taught by Enoch. (Story setting)................PGP, Moses 7:10-11
The gospel taught by Noah. (Story setting).................PGP, Moses 8:23-24

Related References: **Related References**

This the dispensation of the fulness of time...................D&C 112:30-32........
A welding together of dispensations and keys.................D&C 128:18.............

See also APOSTASY.

Preached without Charge

Objective: To show that authorized representatives of the Church of Jesus Christ teach the gospel without charge.

Bible: **Bible**

The hireling careth not for the sheep..............................John 10:11-13...........
These hands have ministered unto my necessities..........Acts 20:33-34...........
Paul preached the gospel of Christ without charge........1 Cor. 9:18...............
A bishop not to be greedy for filthy lucre......................1 Tim. 3:3................
Feed the flock not for filthy lucre..................................1 Pet. 5:2...............

Latter Day Scripture: **Latter Day Scripture**

Mosiah labored with his own hands. (Story setting)....Mosiah 2:10-19........
Priests commanded to labor for their own support........Mosiah 18:24-26........
They were all equal, and they did all labor.....................Alma 1:26................
Alma labored with his own hands. (Story setting)........Alma 30:32-34..........

Related References: **Related References**

Note. Paul was instrumental in making a collection to aid the poor Saints at Jerusalem (Acts 11:29; Rom. 15:26; 1 Cor. 16:1). He also received assistance from the Saints occasionally to sustain his personal needs (Philip. 4:15-16), this being in harmony with Jesus' instructions to the Twelve (Matt. 10:9-10). Beyond this, however, his testimony stands that he did not preach the gospel for charge (1 Cor. 9:18).

HELL

Between Death and the Resurrection

Objective: To show that in the spirit world after death the wicked inherit a state of torment. From this state all but a few will in due time find deliverance after they have paid the full penalty for their sins.

Bible:

	Bible
Thou wilt not leave my soul in hell	Psalm 16:9-11
The rich man and Lazarus. (Note. The gulf referred to was bridged by Christ)	Luke 16:19-31
Christ preached to the spirits in prison. (The possibility of deliverance is clearly implied. Comp. D&C 76:71-74)	1 Pet. 3:18-20
Death and hell (the finally unredeemed partakers thereof at the last resurrection) to deliver up dead and be cast into second death. (Compare 2 Nephi 9:10-16)	Rev. 20:12-15
All wicked to have *their part* in second death. (See Note 2)	Rev. 21:8

Latter Day Scripture:

	Latter Day Scripture
Paradise and hell to deliver up spirits	2 Nephi 9:10-16
State of soul after death. (Story setting, ch. 39)	Alma 40:11-14
All wicked to have *their part* in second death. (See Note 2)	D&C 63:17
Some to be "thrust down to hell" till the last resurrection, then redeemed and given telestial glory	D&C 76:81-85
Righteous at Savior's coming caught up. The wicked to wait. Some to be filthy at the end	D&C 88:95-102
Wicked of Noah's time in torment till Christ	PofGP, Moses 7:38-39
Enoch foresees redemption of spirits in prison	PofGP, Moses 7:55-57

Related References:

	Related References
Eternal and endless punishment explained	D&C 19:4-13

For further concerning redemption from the spirit world hell, see SALVATION FOR THE DEAD.

After the Resurrection

Objective: To show that the ultimate hell — from which the possibility of escape has never been revealed — exists in the resurrection as the inheritance of a class called sons of perdition.

Bible: **Bible**

Some to awake to everlasting life, some to shame..........Dan. 12:2..................
All to be resurrected to life or damnation.
   (See Note 3 following "Resurrection
   of Mankind."   RESURRECTION)....................John 5:28-29..............
Death and hell (the finally unredeemed par-
   takers thereof at the last resurrection)
   to deliver up dead and be cast into sec-
   ond death. (Compare 2 Nephi 9:10-16)...................Rev. 20:12-15...........

Latter Day Scripture: **Latter Day Scripture**

Men to be judged by works. Filthy inherit hell............1 Nephi 15:30-36......
Followers of Devil to go into torment............................2 Nephi 9:10-16........
Those who shall be cast into endless torment.................Jacob 6:8-10.............
Hell is *like* an unquenchable fire. (Story setting)..........Mosiah 2:36-39........
Resurrection and second death. (Story setting)............Alma 12:12-18..........
Righteous to have eternal life; wicked, hell..................D&C 29:26-29..........
The fall, spiritual death, and final damnation................D&C 29:40-45..........
Wicked to go into fire. Their end no man knows..........D&C 43:33...............
Sons of perdition. Only ones on whom sec-
   ond death to have any (enduring) power.
   (See also note following "Sin Against
   the Holy Ghost."   HOLY GHOST)...............D&C 76:31-49..........
Four kingdoms; three of glory, one not of glory............D&C 88:22-35..........

Related References: **Related References**

Eternal and endless punishment explained.....................D&C 19:4-13...........

Note 1. It is to be understood that none of the degrees of glory is hell; they are degrees *of glory*, heavens all three (Compare 2 Cor. 12:2). Though persons who inherit one of the inferior degrees presumably may experience a type of "hell" through a realization of lost opportunity, the *kingdom of hell* itself is a place apart (Compare D&C 88:22-35).

Note 2. The second death is not annihilation of the soul but a death "pertaining unto righteousness" (Alma 12:16; also v. 32). As such it is experienced, in part, by all the wicked (Rev. 21:8, D&C 63:17) while in their spirit state before the final resurrection. Upon sons of perdition only, however, is it ultimately binding (D&C 76:37).

For further concerning degrees of glory in the resurrection, see "Three Degrees of Glory." RESURRECTION.

For further concerning the identity of sons of perdition, see "Sin Against the Holy Ghost." HOLY GHOST.

HEREAFTER

Objective: To show that between death and the resurrection, though the body sleeps, the spirit continues an active conscious existence in a world of spirits.

Bible: **Bible**

Rich man and Lazarus. (Note. The "gulf"
  referred to was bridged by Christ).....................Luke 16:19-31...........
Today shalt thou be in paradise. (Story setting).........Luke 23:42-43...........
Existence of spirits implied. "A spirit hath not".......Luke 24:36-43...........
Jesus preached to the spirits in prison.............................1 Pet. 3:18-20...........

Latter Day Scripture: **Latter Day Scripture**

Paradise and hell to deliver up spirits...........................2 Nephi 9:12-13.......
State of soul after death. (Story setting, Ch. 39).........Alma 40:11-14..........
Spirits regard absence from bodies as bondage...............D&C 45:17...............

Related References: **Related References**

Keys by which spirits may be known.............................D&C 129...................
All spirit is matter, but it is more fine or pure...............D&C 131:7-8...........

Note. Ecclesiastes 9:4-10 has been used by some to show that all existence ends at death.
The statement is clarified by the writer in Ecclesiastes 12:7.
See also "Gospel Preached to the Dead by Christ." SALVATION FOR THE DEAD.
Concerning the workings of deceiving spirits, see "Miracles Alone Not Proof of True
Church. SPIRITUAL GIFTS.

HOLY GHOST

What It Is

Objective: To show that the Holy Ghost is a member of the Godhead and a personage of spirit separate in identity from the Father and the Son.

Bible: **Bible**

Holy Ghost one of the Trinity. (Story setting)............Matt. 3:16-17...........
Sin against the Holy Ghost different from sin
  against the Son. (Separate beings indicated).........Matt. 12:31-32..........
Baptism in the name of the Three. (Story setting).....Matt. 28:19................

Latter Day Scripture: **Latter Day Scripture**

Spirit of Lord in form of a man. (Story setting).........1 Nephi 11:10-11......
The Holy Ghost a personage of spirit..............................D&C 130:22.............

Related References: **Related References**

The Holy Ghost was in existence before the time
  of Christ. (Compare Luke 1:41, 2 Peter 1:21).......Acts 1:16....................

Necessary for All to Receive

Objective: To show that the baptism (confirmation) of the Holy Ghost is essential to salvation.

Bible:	Bible
He shall baptize with Holy Ghost. (Story setting)	Matt. 3:11
Jesus receives heavenly confirmation	Matt. 3:13-17
Born of water and of the *Spirit*. (Story setting)	John 3:5
The Holy Ghost descends upon the apostles	Acts 2:1:4
Promise of Holy Ghost to all. (Story setting)	Acts 2:37-39
Given to them that obey Him. (Story setting)	Acts 5:32
Ananias sent to confirm Paul. (Story setting)	Acts 9:17

Latter Day Scripture	Latter Day Scripture
Reception of Holy Ghost only the gateway	2 Nephi 31:17-21
After faith, repentance, and baptism comes the gift	D&C 49:11-14
The Holy Spirit necessary for celestial glory	D&C 76:50-53
Adam receives heavenly confirmation	PGP, Moses 6:65-68
Holy Ghost promised by Noah. (Story setting)	PGP, Moses 8:23-24

Related References:	Related References
Jesus gives power to confirm. (Comp. Moroni 2:1-3)	3 Nephi 18:36-37

Conferred by the Laying on of Hands

Objective: To show that the gift of the Holy Ghost is conferred — following water baptism — by the laying on of hands of those having authority.

Bible:	Bible
Peter and John lay on hands. (Story setting)	Acts 8:14-20
Paul confers Holy Ghost by laying on of hands	Acts 19:1-6
Repentance, faith, baptism, *laying on of hands*	Heb. 6:1-2

Latter Day Scripture:	Latter Day Scripture
Authority given by Christ to bestow Holy Ghost	Moroni 2:1-3
Holy Ghost conferred by laying on of hands	D&C 49:11-14
Laying on of hands needed for celestial glory	D&C 76:50-53

Related References:	Related References
Holy Ghost may descend on one and not tarry	D&C 130:23
Joseph Smith was visited with Holy Ghost temporarily before the laying on of hands. (Story setting)	PGP, Smith 2:73

Gifts and Functions

Objective: To show that the Holy Ghost has numerous gifts that are given to
bless men according to their worthiness and needs.

Bible:	Bible
The Holy Ghost a comforter and teacher	John 14:26
The Comforter to testify of Jesus	John 15:26
To guide into all truth and show things to come	John 16:13-14
The Holy Ghost a witness for Christ. (Story setting)	Acts 5:30-32
Gift of tongues, prophecy. (Story setting)	Acts 19:6
Gift of prophecy. "Thus saith the Holy Ghost"	Acts 21:10-12
Diversities of gifts: wisdom, knowledge, faith	1 Cor. 12:1-11
Fruits of the Spirit: love, joy, peace, goodness	Gal. 5:22-23

Latter Day Scripture:	Latter Day Scripture
Repentance, baptism. The Holy Ghost and its gifts	Moroni 8:25-26
Truth given by Holy Ghost. Gifts enumerated	Moroni 10:4-19
Spirit of revelation by the Holy Ghost	D&C 8:2-3
Teacheth the peaceable things of the kingdom	D&C 39:6
Gifts of the Spirit enumerated	D&C 46:13-29

Related References:	Related References
Gift of tongues not given to cause confusion	1 Cor. Chap. 14
Whatever spoken through Holy Ghost, scripture	D&C 68:3-4

See also SPIRITUAL GIFTS.

Sin Against the Holy Ghost

Objective: To show that he who willfully chooses evil after having received
a perfect knowledge of the truth commits blasphemy against the Holy Ghost,
for which there is no pardon.

Bible:	Bible
Blasphemy against Holy Ghost not forgiven	Matt. 12:31-32
Enlightened, who fall away, cannot be renewed	Heb. 6:4-6
There remaineth no more sacrifice for sins	Heb. 10:26-29
There is a sin unto death	1 John 5:16

Latter Day Scripture:	Latter Day Scripture
Ye must go away into that lake of fire	Jacob 6:8-10
"I denied the Christ." (Story setting)	Jacob 7:19
Rebellion against God brings torment. (Story setting)	Mosiah 2:36-39
A sin which is unpardonable. (Story setting)	Alma 39:6
Fate of the sons of perdition. (See note below)	D&C 76:31-49
Breaking priesthood covenant not forgiven	D&C 84:40-41
Murder and the sin against the Holy Ghost	D&C 132:27

Related References: **Related References**

   None of them is lost but the son of perdition..................John 17:12-13............

Note. That the resurrection will come to all is not denied by Doctrine and Covenants 76:39 as pertaining to the sons of perdition. Their coming forth simply does not represent "the triumph and glory of the Lamb," v. 39. The scriptures are explicit, however, that they and all others shall be resurrected. John 5:28-29; Alma 11:41-44; D&C 29:26-28; D&C 88:22-35.

For further concerning the final doom of the unredeemed see "After the Resurrection." HELL.

JUDGMENT

Judgment at Christ's Coming

Objective: To show that the second coming of Jesus Christ will be a day of judgment which will bring about a general separation of the wicked from the righteous.

Bible: **Bible**

   Christ to come that He may judge his people................Psalm 50:3-6.............

   Christ to come with Ancient of Days to judge.............Dan. 7:9-14................

   The day cometh that shall burn as an oven...................Mal. 4:1-3.................

   Parable of the tares explained. (Story setting)............Matt. 13:40-43*.......

   Son to come and reward all according to works............Matt. 16-27.............

   Twelve apostles to judge tribes of Israel.....................Matt. 19:28†...........

   Judgment at Coming to separate sheep from goats.......Matt. 25:31-46‡.......

   Vengeance to fall on disobedient at Christ's Coming.......2 Thess. 1:7-10..........

   The Lord cometh to execute judgment.........................Jude 14-15.................

   Fate of good and bad at the coming of Christ...............Rev. 20:4-6§.............

Latter Day Scripture: **Latter Day Scripture**

   Twelve apostles to judge house of Israel........................D&C 29:12-13†........

   Ye Saints arise; ye sinners stay and sleep.....................D&C 43:17-19...........

   At that hour cometh an entire separation.......................D&C 63:54................

   Parable of the wheat and the tares explained.................D&C 86:1-7*.............

   Fate of living and dead at coming of Christ..................D&C 88:86-110‡§....

   Separation of wheat from tares at Coming.....................D&C 101:65-66........

Related References: **Related References**

Note. Passages applicable equally to "Judgment at Christ's Coming" and "The Final Judgment" are listed under Related References of "The Final Judgment."

For further concerning events to transpire at the Savior's coming, see "Christ's Coming Foretold." SECOND COMING OF JESUS CHRIST.

The Final Judgment

Objective: To show that a great and last judgment will come at the end of the Millennium, at which time all men will receive their eternal reward according to their works.

Bible:	Bible
(Devil's) angels reserved in chains unto judgment	Jude 6
"And I saw the dead." The final judgment	Rev. 20:12-13*†

Latter Day Scripture:	Latter Day Scripture
Men judged by works. Filthy inherit hell	1 Nephi 15:30-36
Death, hell, and final judgment before God	2 Nephi 9:10-19*
The narrow way. Wicked to admit guilt	2 Nephi 9:41-46
All shall stand before God. (Story setting)	Alma 12:12-15
All things justly restored. (Story setting, Ch. 39)	Alma 41:1-7
And then cometh the judgment of the Holy One	Mormon 9:12-14
Satan's works to be destroyed at the judgment day	D&C 19:3
Michael to sound his trump; all to come forth	D&C 29:26-28
Residue of wicked kept till judgment at the end	D&C 38:5-6
Fate of the earth and its inhabitants explained	D&C 88:25-35

Related References:	Related References
Many will say to Me in that day, "Lord, Lord"	Matt. 7:21-23
Men to answer for every idle word at judgment	Matt. 12:36-37
Unto whomsoever much is given is much required	Luke 12:47-48
Righteous to receive glory; wicked, misery	Rom. 2:3-8
We shall all stand before the judgment-seat	Rom. 14:10-13
All must answer for deeds at judgment day	2 Cor. 5:10
Where there is no law there is no punishment	2 Nephi 9:25-27
Judged out of the books. (Story setting)	3 Nephi 27:23-24†
Judgment by works. Role of Nephite Twelve	Mormon 3:18-22

For further concerning rewards and punishments received through the judgment, see "Three Degrees of Glory." RESURRECTION. See also "After the Resurrection." HELL.

LATTER DAY REVELATION

Revelation

Objective: To establish the necessity of divine revelation and to show how and by whom it may be received.

Bible:	Bible
Where there is no vision the people perish	Prov. 29:18
The Lord's secrets revealed to prophets	Amos 3:7
Upon this rock (testimony, prophecy) I will build My Church. (Compare Rev. 19:10)	Matt. 16:13-19
Things of God known only by the Spirit of God	1 Cor. 2:9-11

Saints should desire the gift of prophecy..........................1 Cor. 14:1..............
Prophecy common in Church in Paul's day...................1 Cor. 14:29-31..........
Paul prays Saints may have spirit of revelation.............Eph. 1:15-17.............
Quench not the Spirit. Despise not prophecy...............1 Thess. 5:19-20........
Wisdom from above given. "If any of you lack"......James 1:5-6...............
Sure word of prophecy. Had also in times of old........2 Pet. 1:19-21...............
Last book of the Bible, a record of revelations..............Rev. 1:1..................
Testimony of Jesus is the spirit of prophecy.................Rev. 19:10.................

Latter Day Scripture: **Latter Day Scripture**

God is able to speak to men on the earth.......................Jacob 4:8-10............
Seer, revelator, prophet defined. (Story setting)...........Mosiah 8:13-18..........
This is the spirit of revelation......................................D&C 8:2-3................
Revelation and translation. "Your bosom shall burn"....D&C 9:7-9................
Revelation for Church through prophet head.................D&C 43:2-7..............
Greater revelations bring responsibilities........................D&C 82:2-4..............
President of Church, a prophet, seer, revelator.............D&C 107:91-92........
Kinds of messengers. How to distinguish....................D&C 129.................

Related References: **Related References**

Concerning the workings of deceiving spirits, see "Miracles Alone Not Proof of True Church." SPIRITUAL GIFTS.

The Visitation of Angels

Objective: To show that Joseph Smith's description and claims concerning the visitation of heavenly messengers is in full harmony with the testimony of scripture.

Bible: **Bible**

Two angels appear to Lot. (Story setting)....................Gen. 19:1-3.............
Moses and Elias (Elijah) appear to Jesus.......................Matt. 17:1-9............
Many beings appear after Jesus' resurrection..............Matt. 27:52-53........
Angel rolls back stone from Jesus' grave......................Matt. 28:1-8.............
An angel comes to Zacharias and Mary. (Story)........Luke 1:11-28.............
Two men (angels, v. 23) at Jesus' grave. (Story)........Luke 24:1-4...............
Two men (angels) present at Jesus' ascension...............Acts 1:9-11..............
An angel frees Peter from prison. (Story setting)........Acts 12:7-10..........
An angel appears to Paul. (Story setting)....................Acts 27:21-26...........
Some have entertained angels unawares...........................Heb. 13:2...............
Angel tells John, "I am thy fellowservant".....................Rev. 19:10.................

Latter Day Scripture: **Latter Day Scripture**

Elijah, Moses, others appear. (Story setting)...............D&C 110....................
Kinds of messengers. How to distinguish....................D&C 129.................
Angels belong to earth. Live on another globe............D&C 130:4-7............
The Angel Moroni described. (Story setting)...............PGP, Smith 2:30-32

Related References: **Related References**

Revelation Later Than the Bible Predicted

Objective: To show that latter day revelation — as claimed by Mormonism —
is in direct harmony with the promises of scripture.

Bible: **Bible**

God to speak to gathered Israel "face to face"	Ezek. 20:33-37
God to set up kingdom in *latter days*. (Chapter)	Dan. 2:26-45
Messenger to precede Lord's coming in glory	Mal. 3:1-3
Behold, I will send you Elijah the prophet	Mal. 4:5-6*
Spirit of the Lord to be poured out upon all flesh in the last days. (Story setting.) Also Joel 2:28-32	Acts 2:17
A restitution of all things. (Story setting)	Acts 3:19-21
Two mighty prophets to *prophesy* and suffer martyrdom in Jerusalem at the time of the end	Rev. 11:1-15
An angel to bring the gospel and sound important warning: "The hour of God's judgment is come"	Rev. 14:6-7†
A voice from heaven to proclaim gathering	Rev. 18:4-8‡

Latter Day Scripture: **Latter Day Scripture**

Woe to them who say they have enough	2 Nephi 28:29-30
Other records than Bible promised	2 Nephi 29:3-14
Greater things than Book of Mormon to come	3 Nephi 26:8-10
Three Nephites to appear. (Story setting)	3 Nephi 28:25-32
All mysteries to be revealed to righteous	D&C 76:5-10
Elijah comes and confers keys. (Story setting)	D&C 110:13-16*
A time to come in which nothing to be withheld	D&C 121:26-32
Revelation on gathering. (Also D&C 29:7-8)	D&C 133:6-15‡
Gospel and warning brought by angel (Moroni)	D&C 133:36-39†
Prophet's first latter day revelations told	PofGP, Smith 2

Related References: **Related References**

Note 1. Occasionally objection to latter day revelation is sustained in the view that John the Baptist was meant to be the world's last prophet. (See Luke 16:16.) That prophets came after John and were, indeed, vital in Christ's Church is made clear by numerous passages. Luke 11:49-50; Acts 21:10; 1 Cor. 14:1; 1 Cor. 14:29-31; Eph. 4:11; Rev. 11:3-10.

Note 2. In Revelation 22:18-19 John forbade men to add to or take from "this book" (of Revelation). This, of course, does not restrict God, else similar injunctions in Deuteronomy 4:2 and 12:32 would require that the greater part of the Bible itself be rejected.

Note 3. A sufficient reason for latter day revelation and scripture is the fact that the Bible is not complete. See MISSING SCRIPTURE.

MAN'S FREE AGENCY

Objective: To show that: (a) earth life is a place in which opposing forces of evil and good and the freedom to choose between them are essential elements in the scheme for man's progress; (b) man is free to choose for himself and is, therefore, properly held to strict accountability for his acts.

Bible: **Bible**

Adam commanded not to eat fruit of tree......................Gen. 2:16-17*...........
Choosing to honor parents to bring long life..................Ex. 20:12................
I set before you a blessing and a curse.........................Deut. 11:26-28.........
Choice given of life and good or death and evil............Deut. 30:15-19.........
Choose you this day whom ye will serve.......................Josh. 24:14-15...........
How long halt ye between two
    opinions? (Story setting).....................................1 Kings 18:21............
Decreed fall of Nineveh changed by repentance.............Jonah Chaps. 1-4......
Twelve free to forsake Christ. "Will ye also go?".......John 6:66-68..............
Whatsoever a man soweth that shall he reap................Gal. 6:7-8.................

Latter Day Scripture: **Latter Day Scripture**

Opposition necessary to man's free agency (Chapter)......2 Nephi 2:11, 15-16..
Men free to choose liberty or captivity...........................2 Nephi 2:27.............
Fall put man in a state to act. (Story setting).............Alma 12:31................
God allotteth to men according to their wills..................Alma 29:4-5..............
Judged by desires and works. (Story setting, Ch. 39)...Alma 41:3-7..............
Ye are free; permitted to act. (Story setting, Ch. 13)...Helaman 14:30-31....
Without temptation men could not be agents................D&C 29:35-39............
Men should do many things of their free will..............D&C 58:26-29............
Through agency every man accountable for sins...........D&C 101:78-80.........
Priesthood not to be used to compel men.....................D&C 121:41-44.........
Adam commanded not to eat but given choice...............PGP, Moses 3:16-17*
Satan's plan sought to destroy man's agency.................PGP, Moses 4:1-4....
Man given agency in the Garden of Eden....................PGP, Moses 7:32......
Earth life a testing ground. "We will prove them".......PGP, Abrm. 3:24-26

Related References: **Related References**

All truth independent to act for itself.............................D&C 93:30-31..........
Laws should protect free conscience.............................D&C 134:2 ....

Note. The promise that men will be rewarded according to their works presupposes in-
dividual freedom to choose good or evil deeds. See JUDGMENT.

MARRIAGE

Objective: To show that marriage is honorable and, when performed by
    divine authority, is a union that endures for eternity.

Bible: **Bible**

Be fruitful and multiply and replenish earth..................Gen. 1:26-28.............
It is not good for the man to be alone...........................Gen. 2:18.................
God institutes the first marriage. (Comp. Eccl. 3:14)...Gen. 2:21-24.............
Power to bind and loose promised. (Story setting)......Matt. 16:19*............
What God hath joined let no man put asunder.............Matt. 19:3-8...............
Peter was married; his "wife's mother".......................Luke 4:38.................
Neither is the man without the woman........................1 Cor. 11:11-12..........

Woman shall be saved in childbearing.............................1 Tim. 2:15.............
Paul says bishops, deacons should be married...............1 Tim. 3:1-12...........
Paul warns of some who will forbid to marry................1 Tim. 4:1-3............
I will that the younger women marry..........................1 Tim. 5:14..............
Marriage is honorable in all...................................Heb. 13:4...............

Latter Day Scripture: **Latter Day Scripture**

Marriage is ordained of God unto man..........................D&C 49:15-17...........
Highest place in celestial possible only for married........D&C 131:1-4...........
Marriage law and its eternal nature revealed..................D&C 132...............
Power to seal restored through the priesthood.............D&C 132:45-46*.......

Related References: **Related References**

Isaac and Rebekah. The choosing of a mate.................Gen. Chap. 24.........
David transgresses the marriage covenant....................2 Sam. 11, 12:1-14....
No marrying in resurrection. (Comp. D&C 132:15-18)....Matt. 22:23-30.........
Men to have one wife unless God commands.................Jacob 2:27-30..........
Lamanites more loyal in marriage than Nephites...........Jacob 3:5-11............
Immorality condemned. Second only to murder...........Alma 39:3-5...........
Marriage vows to be kept. Penalty for adultery...........D&C 42:24-26.........

Note. A problem of interpretation is raised by the Apostle Paul's counsel regarding marriage in I Corinthians, Chapter 7. From the King James text it would appear that his point of view is not unmixed with opinion. (See verses 6, 12, 25, 40.) That elsewhere his endorsement of marriage is positive and unmistakable is plain from certain passages cited above.

MILLENNIUM

See CHRIST'S REIGN ON EARTH

MISSING SCRIPTURE

Objective: To show that, since valuable parts of the Bible are missing, it is reasonable that God should give mankind additional scripture in these latter days.

Bible: **Bible**

Book of the Covenant..Ex. 24:7................
Book of the Wars of the Lord...................................Num. 21:14.............
Book of Jasher...Josh. 10:13.............
A book of statutes..1 Sam. 10:25...........
Book of the Acts of Solomon.....................................1 Kings 11:41.........
Books of Nathan and Gad...1 Chron. 29:29.........
Prophecy of Ahijah and Visions of Iddo......................2 Chron. 9:29..........
Book of Shemaiah..2 Chron. 12:15........
Book of Jehu...2 Chron. 20:34.......
Acts of Uzziah...2 Chron. 26:22........
Sayings of the Seers...2 Chron. 33:19........
An earlier epistle of Paul to the Corinthians.................1 Cor. 5:9..............

Another epistle of Paul to the Ephesians.........................Eph. 3:3....................
An epistle of Paul from Laodicea....................................Col. 4:16....................
Former epistle of Jude...Jude 3.........................
Prophecies of Enoch..Jude 14......................

Latter Day Scripture: **Latter Day Scripture**

Many plain and precious parts taken from Bible............1 Nephi 13:24-29......
Many gospel truths restored in Book of Mormon..........1 Nephi 13:34-35......
Latter day scriptures a witness for the Bible.................1 Nephi 13:38-40......
Lord gives line upon line, precept upon precept.............2 Nephi 28:29-30......
Many unknown scriptures: "I command all men"........2 Nephi 29:3-14......
One like Moses to give world lost writings....................Moses 1:40-41............
A book of remembrance kept in the days of Adam........Moses 6:5-6................

Related References: **Related References**

Only part of what Jesus said in the Bible.......................John 21:25................
Whatever spoken through Holy Ghost is scripture........D&C 68:3-4................

NEW JERUSALEM

Objective: To show that the city of Zion, New Jerusalem, is destined to be
built upon this (the American) continent by the Saints of God prior to the
second coming of Jesus Christ.

Bible: **Bible**

When Lord shall build up Zion He shall appear.............Psalm 102:16............
Out of Zion to go law; word of the Lord, Jerusalem........Isa. 2:2-3....................
The city of the living God, the heavenly Jerusalem......Heb. 12:22................
New Jerusalem which cometh out of heaven.................Rev. 3:12*................
Description of the New Jerusalem given.........................Rev. Chap. 21..........

Latter Day Scripture: **Latter Day Scripture**

A New Jerusalem to be built in America........................3 Nephi 20:22............
God's people to gather to New Jerusalem.......................3 Nephi 21:20-25......
New Jerusalem in America. Old Jerusalem rebuilt.......Ether 13:4-11*............
New Jerusalem to be a refuge for the Saints..................D&C 45:66-67............
Site of New Jerusalem and temple revealed...................D&C 57:1-3................
After much tribulation come the blessings.....................D&C 58:3-4................
Temple to be reared in this generation...........................D&C 84:2-5................
The nations of the earth to honor city of Zion...............D&C 97:19-20..........
The gathering to New Jerusalem. Christ's coming........PGP, Moses 7:60-66

Related References: **Related References**

A holy city built by Enoch anciently...............................PGP, Moses 7:18-21

For passages dealing with both the New Jerusalem and the old see "Two Gathering
Places." GATHERING OF ISRAEL.

PERSECUTION

Objective: To show that: (a) Joseph Smith's persecution and martyrdom — by its similarity to the treatment accorded the prophets of old — commands attention to the claim that he was a prophet of God; (b) those who are persecuted for the gospel's sake will be blessed.

Bible: **Bible**

Men blessed when persecuted for righteousness.............Matt. 5:10-12............

Convert's foes to be of own household...........................Matt. 10:34-36.........

Hated of all nations for my name's sake........................Matt. 24:9

Enemies to kill Saints and think they serve God...........John 16:1-3.................

The prophets always persecuted. (Story setting).........Acts 7:51-52................

Christian sect everywhere spoken against. (Story)......Acts 28:22..................

Paul's sufferings for the gospel accounted....................2 Cor. 11:24-27........ .

All that live godly to suffer persecution........................2 Tim. 3:12................

Great sufferings to the ancients told..............................Heb. 11:36-38............

Whom the Lord loveth He chasteneth.............................Heb. 12:6-7................

Early martyrs to be joined by later ones........................Rev. 6:9-11................

Latter Day Scripture: **Latter Day Scripture**

Abinadi burned alive. (Story setting)............................Mosiah 17:6-20..........

Alma, Amulek see Saints burned. (Story setting)........Alma 14:9-13.............

Persecution of Saints again breaks out..........................4 Nephi 1:27-34........

Law of forgiveness and resistance given.........................D&C 98:23-48...........

Those who die for Christ to obtain glory........................D&C 101:35-36........

The Prophet's prison prayer and persecutions.................D&C 121:1-25...........

Trials of Joseph Smith designed for own good................D&C 122:5-8............

The Prophet's comment on his perils..............................D&C 127:2-3.............

Martyrdom of Prophet Joseph and Hyrum told............D&C 135...................

"For they killed the prophets." Woes to come..............D&C 136:34-36........

The Prophet persecuted for his

    testimony. (Story setting)...PGP, Smith 2:23-25

Related References: **Related References**

Note. In his *Book of the Martyrs* George Fox accounts for the death or exile of the early Church leaders as follows:

Peter was crucified at Rome, head downward. James (the son of Zebedee) was beheaded. John was banished. Bartholomew was flayed alive. Judas committed suicide. James (the son of Alphaeus) was beaten to death. Matthew was slain with a battle ax. Andrew and Simon were crucified. Philip was hanged (or crucified). Thaddeus was shot to death with arrows. Thomas was run through with a lance. Matthias was stoned and then beheaded. Paul was beheaded in Rome by Nero. Barnabas was stoned by the Jews.

PERSONALITY OF GOD

God a Personal Being

Objective: To show that God is an embodied personal being in whose very image man was created.

Bible:

Bible	
Man created in God's image. (Compare Gen. 5:3)	Gen. 1:26-27
"I have seen God face to face." (Story setting)	Gen. 32:30
Moses and seventy elders of Israel see God	Ex. 24:9-11
The Lord speaks to Moses "face to face"	Ex. 33:9-11
God's hand, back parts, and face mentioned	Ex. 33:21-23
Similitude of Lord shall he behold. (Story setting)	Num. 12:5-8
Stephen sees Father and Son. (Story setting)	Acts. 7:55-56
Christ the express image of His Father's person	Heb. 1:1-3
Men made after the similitude of God	James 3:8-9
Righteous promised they shall see God's face	Rev. 22:3-6

Latter Day Scripture:

Latter Day Scripture	
The Lord reveals Himself to the brother of Jared	Ether Chap. 3
Jehovah appears in Kirtland temple (Note v. 3)	D&C 110:1-10
Father and Son have bodies of flesh and bone	D&C 130:22
Moses sees God face to face. (Chapter)	PGP, Moses 1:1-11
Joseph Smith sees Father and Son. (Story setting)	PGP, Smith 2:15-19

Related References:

Related References	
Thou shalt have no other Gods before Me	Ex. 20:3
The fool hath said in his heart, "There is no God"	Psalm 14:1
Thou shalt love the Lord thy God. (Story setting)	Matt. 22:37-39
God is a spirit. (As man also is, D&C 93:33)	John 4:24
This is life eternal to know God. (Story setting)	John 17:3
We are the offspring of God. (Story setting)	Acts 17:29-30
No man hath seen God at any time. (For meaning see D&C 67:10-12; PofGP, Moses 1:11)	1 John 4:12
All things denote there is a God. (Story setting)	Alma 30:44

Note 1. The Israelites were told that they could not see God's face, ". . . for there shall no man see Me and live." (Exodus 33:20.) The fulness of God's presence was withheld from Israel at this time because they had hardened their hearts. (D&C 84:21-25; Exodus 32:30-35.) That both earlier and later certain men were permitted to see His face is shown by passages cited above.

See THE PREMORTAL GODSHIP OF CHRIST. Appendix Note 1.

Concerning the personal corporeal identity of Jesus Christ after His resurrection, see "Resurrection of Christ." RESURRECTION.

Attributes of God

Objective: To show that God is a merciful, kind, and loving Father, eternal, unchangeable, just, all-wise, all-present, all powerful; the supreme example of the perfection mankind should strive to attain.

Bible:

	Bible
A jealous and merciful God. (10 Commandments)	Ex. 20:4-6
Merciful, gracious, longsuffering. (Story setting)	Ex. 34:6-7
A God of love; faithful and merciful	Deut. 7:7-9
God capable of righteous indignation. His anger	Judges 2:14
God ready to pardon, slow to anger, and kind	Neh. 9:17
God's spirit omni-present. "Whither shall I go?"	Psalm 139:7-10
The Book of Jonah, a story of God's universal love	Jonah Chaps. 1-4
God is perfect. "Be ye therefore perfect"	Matt. 5:48
A God of love. "For God so loved the world"	John 3:16-17
God is love. To dwell in love is to dwell in God	1 John 4:7-8
Lord all-powerful. "God omnipotent reigneth"	Rev. 19:6

Latter Day Scripture:

	Latter Day Scripture
God's love depicted in vision. (Story setting)	1 Nephi 11:21-23
Christ's love beautifully shown in Nephite visit	3 Nephi Chap. 17
God is infinite, eternal, unchangeable	D&C 20:17-19
The same which knoweth all things	D&C 38:1-3
God's greatness told. He delights to bless	D&C 76:1-5
God is just. "I, the Lord, am bound"	D&C 82:10
The light of Christ fills the immensity of space	D&C 88:6-13
God's majesty. He governs the universe by law	D&C 88:41-50
Christ is the true light. He is one with the Father	D&C 93:1-4
The glory of God is intelligence: light and truth	D&C 93:36
God talks to Moses. His greatness. (Chapter)	PGP, Moses 1:1-11
God's compassion for the wicked shown Enoch	PGP, Moses 7:28-37
I am more intelligent than they all	PofGP, Abrm. 3:19

Related References:

	Related References
Be ye therefore perfect, even as your Father	Matt. 5:48

The Holy Trinity — Three Separate Personages

Objective: To show that the Father, Son, and Holy Ghost are three separate and distinct personal beings.

Bible:

	Bible
Trinity manifest at Jesus' baptism. (Story setting)	Matt. 3:16-17
Sin against the Holy Ghost different from sin against the Son. Separate identities indicated	Matt. 12:31-32
"This is my beloved Son." (Story setting)	Matt. 17:5
Baptism performed in the name of the Three	Matt. 28:19
The Father speaks to the Son. (Story setting)	John 12:28-29
Father and Son are "one," yet separate. (Story setting)	John 17:11, 20-23
"I ascend to My Father." (Story setting)	John 20:17
Stephen sees Father and Son. (Story setting)	Acts 7:55-56
Christ in image of God. Separateness indicated	2 Cor. 4:4
Christ "the image of the invisible God"	Col. 1:12-15

Christ the express image of His Father's person...........Heb. 1:1-3.................

John speaks of "God and his Father" (Note v. 6).........Rev. 1:1-8.................

Latter Day Scripture: **Latter Day Scripture**

Spirit of the Lord in form of a man. (Story setting)....1 Nephi 11:9-11.......

"Behold my Beloved Son." (Story setting)....................3 Nephi 11:7.............

For we saw Him, even on the right hand of God...........D&C 76:22-24.........

Father and Son have tangible bodies of flesh and

    bone. The Holy Ghost is a personage of Spirit........D&C 130:22...............

Joseph Smith sees Father and Son. (Story setting)......PGP, Smith 2:15-19

Related References: **Related References**

"I and My Father are one."

    (Clarified by John 17:11) ....John 10:30...............

Jesus the fulness of the Godhead bodily..........................Col. 2:9....................

Note. Christ in relation to His Father is a Son, for "God the Eternal Father, whom we designate by the exalted name-title 'Elohim' is the literal Father of our Lord and Savior Jesus Christ and of the spirits of the human race"; but in relation to mankind He (Christ), too, occupies the role of "Father" in the sense of (a) "Father" as Creator, (b) "Father" of those who abide in His gospel, and (c) "Father" by divine investiture of authority. See THE FATHER AND THE SON: A DOCTRINAL EXPOSITION BY THE FIRST PRESIDENCY AND THE TWELVE. Appendix Note 2.

Concerning the personal corporeal identity of Jesus Christ after His resurrection, see "Resurrection of Christ." RESURRECTION.

PRAYER

Objective: To show that "the effectual fervent prayer of a righteous man availeth much."

Bible: **Bible**

Pray in secret. Use not vain repetitions.............................Matt. 6:5-8.................

The Lord's prayer. "Our Father which art"................Matt. 6:9-13.............

"Not as I will but as thou wilt. (Story setting)...........Matt. 26:39................

Pray to avoid temptation. The flesh is weak...............Matt. 26:41................

Prayer, belief, and forgiveness. (Story setting)...........Mark 11:24-26.........

"Lord, teach us to pray." Jesus' instructions...............Luke 11:1-13.............

Pray always. Parable of the persistent widow............Luke 18:1-8................

Prayer of the Pharisee and the publican......................Luke 18:9-14.............

Paul counsels Saints to pray without ceasing................1 Thess. 5:17............

If any of you lack wisdom let him ask of God.............James 1:5-6...............

The prayer of faith to save the sick................................James 5:14-15...........

Fervent prayer availeth much. Elias' power...............James 5:16-18...........

Behold, I stand at the door and knock.........................Rev. 3:20...................

Latter Day Scripture: **Latter Day Scripture**

Nephi testifies Lord answers earnest inquirers.............1 Nephi 15:7-11.......

Nephi's great prayer after the death of Lehi.................2 Nephi 4:20-35........

Prayer in the woods of Enos, the hunter......................Enos 1:1-19.............

Call on the Lord daily. Blessings promised.................Mosiah 4:11-12.........

Nephite burdens made light through prayer................Mosiah 24:8-25.........

Angel visits Alma; in answer to prayer, v. 14................Mosiah 27:8-37..........
Prayers of the righteous delay destruction....................Alma 10:22-23..........
Alma's prayer and deliverance from prison....................Alma Chap. 14..........
Spirit of prophecy gained by fasting and prayer............Alma 17:1-3..............
A prayer of form and a prayer of faith. (Chapter)........Alma 31:12-38............
Cry to Him in fields. (Story setting, Alma 32:1-7)........Alma 34:17-28..........
Counsel with the Lord in all thy doings.........................Alma 37:36-37..........
Jesus prays with Nephites to the Father. (Chapter)....3 Nephi 17:13-17......
Jesus instructs Nephites concerning prayer..................3 Nephi 18:15-23......
Prayers of the Nephites and of the Savior....................3 Nephi Chap. 19......
Brother of Jared prays and is visited by the Lord.........Ether Chap. 3..........
Whatever is good to be given when asked in faith.........Moroni 7:26.............
Truth of Book of Mormon may be known by prayer....Moroni 10:4-5............
A burning within or a stupor of thought......................D&C 9:7-9..............
To ask for improper things brings condemnation...........D&C 88:63-65..........
Be humble and the Lord will answer prayers.................D&C 112:10.............
Purity brings confidence. "Let virtue garnish"............D&C 121:45:............
Moses gains strength by prayer, rebukes Satan............PGP, Moses 1:12-25
Joseph Smith's first prayer. (Story setting)..................PGP, Smith 2:15-19
Angel Moroni appears after prayer of faith...................PGP, Smith 2:29-32

Related References:

Related References

I, the Lord, am bound when ye do what I say...............D&C 82:10...............
All blessings are predicated upon law...........................D&C 130:20-21........

For further concerning great works performed through prayer, see "Stories of Faith."
FAITH.

PRE-MORTAL EXISTENCE OF SPIRITS

Christ's Pre-Mortal Existence

Objective: To establish the fact of man's pre-mortal existence by the pre-mortal existence of Christ.

Bible:

Bible

In the beginning was the Word (Christ)........................John 1:1-2, 14............
Jesus to ascend up where He was before........................John 6:38, 51, 62......
Before Abraham was, I am. (Story setting)..................John 8:56-58.............
I came forth from the Father..John 16:28-30............
Christ with Father before the world was.......................John 17:4-5...............
Foreordained before foundation of world......................1 Pet. 1:18-20........   ·

Latter Day Scripture:

Latter Day Scripture

Nephi and Jacob see Savior (over 500 B.C.)..................2 Nephi 11:2-3..........
Christ with Father in beginning. (Story setting)..........3 Nephi 9:15.............
Brother of Jared sees Savior (over 2000 B.C.)..............Ether Chap. 3..........

Related References:

Related References

Man's Pre-Mortal Existence

Objective: To show that: (a) before birth we lived in a pre-mortal world of spirits where we proved ourselves worthy of the experience of mortality; (b) this life is another stage in an eternal purposeful journey.

Bible: **Bible**

Every plant, herb created before it was in the earth......Gen. 2:4-5*...............
God of the spirits of all flesh. (Story setting)...............Num. 16:22................
Pre-mortal life implied. "Where wast thou?"..................Job. 38:4-7...............
The spirit shall *return* unto God who gave it.................Eccl. 12:7.................
Jeremiah appointed to mission before birth....................Jer. 1:4-5.................
Apostles' knowledge of man's existence and ability
    to sin before birth hinted. "Who did sin?".........John 9:1-3.................
God, the Father of spirits..Heb. 12:9.................

Latter Day Scripture: **Latter Day Scripture**

Man in beginning with God. Intelligence eternal..........D&C 93:21-23, 29....
All things created spiritually first.....................................PGP, Moses 3:4-7*..
Abraham shown vision of pre-mortal world...................PGP, Abrm. 3:22-23
Those who kept their first estate were added
    upon. Earth life is a proving ground..............PofGP,
        Abrm. 3:24-26.........

Related References: **Related References**

Nation of birth pre-determined. (Story setting)...........Acts 17:26-27...........
Called according to the foreknowledge of God...............Alma 13:2-4.............

Followers of Satan Cast Out

Objective: To show that the disobedient spirits were denied the privilege of mortality and cast down to earth where, with Satan, they seek continually the downfall of man.

Bible: **Bible**

The angels that sinned cast down to hell.........................2 Pet. 2:4.................
The angels which kept not their first estate....................Jude 6........................
And there was war in heaven. Satan cast out..............Rev. 12:7-12.............

Latter Day Scripture   **Latter Day Scripture**

An angel of God had fallen from heaven..........................2 Nephi 2:17-18......
An angel fell and became the devil....................................2 Nephi 9:8-9...........
A third of the hosts of heaven led away...........................D&C 29:36-38.........
An angel in presence of God thrust down.......................D&C 76:25-28.........
Behold, here am I, send me, I will be thy son...............PGP, Moses 4:1-4...
Satan kept not his first estate. Led away many...........PGP, Abrm. 3:27-28

Related References: **Related References**

How art thou fallen from heaven, Oh Lucifer!...............Isa. 14:12-15.............
Devils recognize Christ. (They once were in heaven)......Mark 3:11-12...........
I beheld Satan as lightning fall from heaven..................Luke 10:17-18...........

_____

_____

Note. That the followers of Satan fully realize their plight in being denied the privilege of mortality is indicated by a number of scriptural instances in which they have sought to gain unlawful possession of physical bodies. Consider especially Mark 5:1-13 and Luke 4:33-35.

RECREATION

Objective: To show that wholesome amusements are proper and pleasing in the sight of God.

Bible: **Bible**

A time for all things. A time to dance...........................Eccles. 3:1-4.............
People to rejoice in the dance..Jer. 31:13................
Jesus accused of pleasure seeking...................................Matt. 11:18-19..........
Jesus attends marriage celebration. (Story setting).....John 2:1-2................

Latter Day Scripture: **Latter Day Scripture**

Lord to be praised with music and dancing..................D&C 136:28.............

Related References: **Related References**

Unto the pure all things are pure....................................Titus 1:15-16...........

_____

_____

_____

REPENTANCE

A Saving Principle

Objective: To show that repentance — consisting of a recognition of guilt, a godly sorrow for sin, and a turning from sin to righteousness — is an essential principle of salvation.

Bible: **Bible**

Let the wicked forsake his way.......................................Isa. 55:6-7................
John the Baptist came preaching repentance.................Matt. 3:1-6..............
Repent; for the kingdom of heaven is at hand..............Matt. 4:17................
Christ came to call sinners to repentance......................Matt. 9:10-13...........
Except ye repent, ye shall all likewise perish................Luke 13:1-5..............
Repent and be baptized. (Story setting).......................Acts 2:37-38............
Repent and be converted. (Story setting).....................Acts 3:19-21............
He commandeth all to repent. (Story setting)..............Acts 17:30................

Godly sorrow worketh repentance to salvation................2 Cor. 7:9-10..............
Repentance, faith, baptism, laying on of hands............Heb. 6:1-2..................
Draw nigh to God. Cleanse hands. Purify hearts........James 4:7-10............
The Lord is willing that all should repent................2 Pet. 3:9...................
No one is without sin. Lord ready to forgive..............John 1:8-9..................
Be zealous and repent. Reward for overcoming............Rev. 3:19-21..............

Latter Day Scripture: **Latter Day Scripture**

If Gentiles repent it shall be well with them....................1 Nephi 14:5-7.........
Days of men prolonged that they might repent.............2 Nephi 2:19-21........
Men must repent and be baptized or be damned...........2 Nephi 9:23-24......
Repentance, humility, and remission of sins...................Mosiah 4:9-12........
As often as My people repent will I forgive..................Mosiah 26:28-32.......
Alma's discourse on repentance. (Chapter)....................Alma 5:27-35...........
Alma's yearning desire to cry repentance....................Alma 29:1-2............
This life is the time to prepare..............................Alma 34:32 35.........
Men not redeemed in sins but from sins..................Helaman 5:9-11........
Blessed are they who will repent and hearken...............Helaman 12:23-26....
Repentance taught by Savior. (Story setting).............3 Nephi 11:32-34....
Men to repent and be baptized (Story setting)...........3 Nephi 27:16-20......
Mormon calls on Gentiles to repent.........................3 Nephi 30:1-2......
America a choice land. People must repent...................Ether 2:9-12..........
Repentance and its fruits told by Moroni.....................Moroni 8:25-26........
No allowance for sin. Forgive-
   ness for penitent. (Section)..............................D&C 1:31-33...........
Inhabitants of earth to repent or be scourged...............D&C 5:19-20...........
The thing of most worth is to teach repentance...........D&C 16:6.............
Worth of souls great. Joy over one that repents.........D&C 18:10-16.........
Lord saves men from suffering if they repent.............D&C 19:15-20.........
After the fall angels proclaimed repentance...................D&C 29:42-45........
Nature in fury soon to declare repentance..................D&C 43:20-29........
Hearken unto My voice lest death overtake you...........D&C 45:2...........
Sins repented of remembered by Lord no more.............D&C 58:42-43........
Repentance and baptism taught to Adam.....................PGP, Moses 6:53-57
Repentance taught by Enoch. (Story setting).............PGP, Moses 7:10-12
Repentance and baptism taught by Noah.....................PGP, Moses 8:20-24

Related References: **Related References**

Blessed he that walks not in counsel of ungodly...........Psalm 1..............
Condemnation that men loved darkness....................John 3:19-21...........
The wages of sin is death................................Rom. 6:23..............
When I would do good evil is present with me.............Rom. 7:19-21.........
Be not deceived. What a man sows he shall reap.........Gal. 6:7-8...........
To know good and do it not is sin........................James 4:17............
Sin is transgression of law. Also Rom. 4:15................1 John 3:4...........
Many to say, "Commit a little sin." Also vs. 20-21......2 Nephi 28:7-8.........
Wickedness never was happiness...........................Alma 41:10...........
Men forget God in prosperity. "Oh, how foolish"........Helaman 12:1-7.......
It is required of men to forgive all who sin...................D&C 64:8-14...........
When forgiveness is no longer required........................D&C 98:23-48.........

Stories of Repentance

Objective: To show, by illustration, that repentance is an essential principle of salvation.

Bible:

Bible

Impenitent cities of Sodom and Gomorrah destroyed for want of ten righteous persons	Gen. 18:20-23.............
	Gen. 19:1-26.............
Jeremiah predicts destruction of Jerusalem except the Jews repent. The Babylonian captivity	Jer. 25:1-14...............
	Jer. 39:1-9*...............
Impenitent Babylon falls before Darius	Dan. Chap. 5................
Fall of Nineveh decreed. Spared by repentance	Jonah Chaps. 1-4......
Joy over sinner that repents. Two parables	Luke 15:3-10..............
Parable of the prodigal son, a repentant sinner	Luke 15:11-32..............
Paul's miraculous conversion and repentance	Acts 9:1-31................

Latter Day Scripture:

Latter Day Scripture

· Lehi calls Jews to repent, predicts captivity	1 Nephi 1:4-20*........
Enos' prayer. His repentance and forgiveness	Enos 1:1-8................
King Benjamin teaches people repentance	Mosiah Chaps. 2, 4-6.............
Nephites repent and escape from enemies	Mosiah Chaps. 21-22.............
Alma's miraculous conversion and repentance	Mosiah Chap. 27......
Alma and Amulek preach repentance to the people of Ammonihah. Their testimony is rejected. The city is destroyed	{ Alma Chap. 8............ Alma 9:12-30............ Alma 16:1-11.............
Repentant Lamanites submit to slaughter	Alma Chap. 24.........
Alma tells of his sinful past and repentance	Alma Chap. 36.........
Brothers encircled by fire. Lamanites repent	Helmaan 5:14-52......
Samuel, the Lamanite prophet, preaches repentance to Nephites. Prophecies fulfilled	{ Helaman Chaps. 13-15............. 3 Nephi Chap. 1........
Nephites repent and gain victory over enemies	3 Nephi Chaps. 3-4...
Signs of Christ's death. Men called to repent	3 Nephi Chaps. 8-10
Story of the downfall of the Jaredite nation through refusal to heed warnings to repent. (Compare Ether 2:9-12)	{ Ether 12:1-4............ Ether 13:13-31.......... Ether Chaps. 14-15..
Impenitent Nephite race destroyed like Jaredites. (Compare Ether 2:9-12)	{ Mormon Chaps. 1-8.. Moroni Chap. 9........

Related References:

Related References

The woman in sin. "Go and sin no more"	John 8:3-11..............

Note. Repentance must continue after baptism. For scripture bearing more directly on this important phase of repentance, see DUTIES OF MEMBERS.

RESTORATION OF THE GOSPEL

Objective: To show that the gospel of Jesus Christ has been restored to earth through the direct ministration of heavenly messengers.

Bible:	Bible
Lord's house established in the last days	Isa. 2:2-3
Kingdom set up by God in *latter days*. (Chapter)	Dan. 2:26-45
A messenger to precede Lord's coming in glory	Mal. 3:1-3
I will send you Elijah the prophet. (Chapter)	Mal. 4:5-6*
Gospel to be preached in all world before the end	Matt. 24:14
A restitution of all things. (Story setting)	Acts 3:19-21
The dispensation of the fullness of times	Eph. 1:10†
An angel to bring the gospel and sound warning: "The hour of God's judgment is come"	Rev. 14:6-7‡

Latter Day Scripture:	Latter Day Scripture
Lost gospel truths restored in Book of Mormon	1 Nephi 13:34-35
A choice seer to be raised up in the latter days	2 Nephi 3:6-15
Scriptures of lost tribes yet to be restored	2 Nephi 29:11-14
The Lord to commence His work among all nations	2 Nephi 30:1-8
Apostleship restored by Peter, James, and John	D&C 27:12-13
Elijah comes to confer keys. (Entire section)	D&C 110:13-16*
This, the dispensation of the fullness of times	D&C 112:30-32†
Restoration events eloquently reviewed	D&C 128:19-21
Gospel and warning brought by angel (Moroni)	D&C 133:36-39‡
The gospel a preparation for great things ahead	D&C 133:57-58
The Father and Son appear. (Story setting)	PofGP, Smith, 2:15-19
The visit of Moroni. Book of Mormon restored	PofGP, Smith, 2:29-60
Aaronic priesthood restored	PofGP, Smith, 2:68-73

Related References:	Related References
A marvelous work and a wonder	Isa. 29:13-14
Elias to restore all things. (Study context)	Matt. 17:11
Until the fullness of the Gentiles be come in	Rom. 11:25
The earth to be restored as it was before	D&C 133:20-25

Note. Suggestive of the timeliness and urgency of the Restoration is Joseph Smith's statement in the Wentworth letter that on the night of the angel Moroni's first visitation the Heavenly Messenger announced "that the time was at hand for the gospel, in all its fullness, to be preached unto all nations *that a people might be prepared for the millennial reign.*" (Compare D&C 133:57-58, cited above.)

RESURRECTION

Resurrection of Christ

Objective: To show the nature of man's resurrection by the resurrection of Jesus Christ.

Bible:

	Bible
Jesus must be killed and be raised again	Matt. 16:21-23
The resurrection announced, "He is risen"	Matt. 28:1-8
Jesus appears to women. "All hail!"	Matt. 28:9-10
Savior appears to disciples on a mountain	Matt. 28:16-20
Jesus predicts His resurrection on third day	Mark 9:31-32
Jesus appears to two disciples on Emmaus Way	Luke 24:13-35
An appearance to Peter. (Compare 1 Cor. 15:5)	Luke 24:34
Jesus appears to His disciples in flesh and bones	Luke 24:36-43
Peter and John find the tomb empty	John 20:1-10
Mary Magdalene sees Savior. "Touch me not"	John 20:11-18
Jesus appears to the convincing of Thomas	John 20:24-31
Jesus appears to His disciples on the seaside	John 21:1-14
Jesus rises to heaven in body. (Com. Luke 24:50-51)	Acts 1:9-11
Stephen sees Father and Son. (Story setting)	Acts 7:55-56
Jesus rises to heaven in body. (Com. Luke 24:50-51)	Acts 10:39-42
The first to rise from the dead. (Story setting)	Acts 26:22-23
Resurrected Lord seen by 500 people at once	1 Cor. 15:3-8
Christ, the firstfruits of them that slept	1 Cor. 15:19-23
The Savior in possession of a "glorious body"	Philip. 3:20-21
The first to rise that He might have preeminence	Col. 1:18
Risen Savior says, "I am alive forevermore"	Rev. 1:18

Latter Day Scripture:

	Latter Day Scripture
Resurrected Lord appears to Nephites	3 Nephi 11:1-17
The final testimony: The risen Christ lives	D&C 76:22-23
Joseph Smith describes resurrected Lord	D&C 110:1-4
When Savior appears we shall see He is a man	D&C 130:1
Father and Son appear in bodily form. (Story setting)	PGP, Smith 2:16-17

Related References:

	Related References
The crucifixion and resurrection story. (Consult also Mark 14-16; Luke 22-24; John 18-21)	Matt. Chaps. 26-28
Christ went to Jews *because* they would kill him	2 Nephi 10:3-5
Events in America at Christ's crucifixion	3 Nephi 8:5-23

Note. The main events of Christ's resurrection cited above may be arranged in a plausible order of occurrence as follows: (1) Matt. 28:1-8; (2) John 20:1-10; (3) John 20:11-18; (4) Luke 24:34; (5) Luke 24:13-32; (6) Luke 24:36-43; (7) John 20:24-31; (8) John 21:1-14; (9) Matt. 28:16-20; (10) Acts 1:9-11; (11) 3 Nephi 11:1-17. Many contemporary Bible students associate the appearance of the five hundred of 1 Cor. 15:6 with the appearance on the mountain of Matt. 28:16-20. Lack of sufficient data prohibits the sequence listing of the appearance to the women of Matt. 28:9-10 and the appearance to James of 1 Cor. 15:7.

Resurrection of Mankind

Objective: To show that every member of the human race will arise from the grave with his body perfectly restored in a state of immortality.

Bible: **Bible**

If a man die shall he live again?.......................................Job 14:14.....................
Job testifies, "In my flesh shall I see God".....................Job 19:25-27...............
He will swallow up death and wipe away tears..............Isa. 25:8.......................
Together with my dead body shall they arise................Isa. 26:19....................
Resurrection represented in vision of dry bones............Ezek. 37:1-14..............
Some to awake to life, some to shame............................Dan. 12:2.....................
Many dead arise upon Jesus' resurrection......................Matt. 27:52-53............
All to be resurrected to life or damnation....................John 5:28-29...............
I am the resurrection and the life. (Story setting).......John 11:25-26............
Resurrection of just and unjust. (Story setting)..........Acts 24:14-15.............
Why should it be thought incredible? (Story setting)...Acts 26:8....................
God hath raised up Lord and will also raise up us.........1 Cor. 6:14................
As in Adam all die, even so in Christ *all* made alive......1 Cor. 15:19-23..........
The last enemy to be destroyed is death. (Chapter)...1 Cor. 15:24-28..........
Death is swallowed up in victory. (Chapter)................1 Cor. 15:51-55..........
Dead in Christ first to rise at Lord's coming................1 Thess. 4:13-17........
Our (resurrected) body to be like Savior's.....................Philip. 3:20-21..........
Resurrection of righteous at coming of Christ..............Rev. 20:4-6*...............
Death and hell to deliver up the dead............................Rev. 20:12-13............

Latter Day Scripture: **Latter Day Scripture**

Death, hell, resurrection, judgment. (Note also v. 4)....2 Nephi 9:10-16†......
Abinadi, on trial, speaks of first resurrection.................Mosiah 15:20-27.......
The body restored to its perfect frame. (Story setting)....Alma 11:42-45..........
Resurrection, judgment; meaning of second death.......Alma 12:12-18..........
The resurrection explained. (Story setting)...................Alma Chap. 40..........
The meaning of restoration...Alma Chap. 41..........
The resurrection of the dead brought by Christ.............Helaman 14:15-18....
Resurrection given to all through Christ.........................Mormon 9:13-14......
Final resurrection of all after Millennium.......................D&C 29:22-28..........
Saints to rise, sinners to sleep on at Christ's coming.....D&C 43:18................
(Worthy) heathens to be in first resurrection.................D&C 45:54................
In Millennium resurrection to be quick change.............D&C 63:49-53..........
Resurrection from dead is redemption of soul................D&C 88:14-16..........
Earth to be quickened; righteous to inherit it.............D&C 88:25-26..........
Resurrection and judgment at coming of Christ...........D&C 88:95-102*........
Body and spirit united receive fullness of joy...............D&C 93:33-34..........
During Millennium men to be changed instantly...........D&C 101:28-31........
This is My work and My glory. (Story setting)...........PGP, Moses 1:39......

Related References: **Related References**

Flesh and blood cannot inherit the kingdom of God.
    (A spiritual substance must replace blood)........1 Cor. 15:50..............
For whom to weep, in view of the resurrection.............D&C 42:45-47.........
Intelligence to rise with men in resurrection..................D&C 130:18-19........

Note 1.   The resurrection of the righteous is termed a first resurrection.   This is doubtless because the righteous are all (or nearly all) brought forth before the resurrection of the wicked begins.

Note 2.   *Immortality* pertains to the state of deathless living that comes to all men through the resurrection.   *Eternal life*, in a theological sense differs from immortality.   (D&C 29:43; D&C 88:4; PofGP. Moses 1:39.)   It is celestial life, the quality of life God metes out to the obedient.   (Compare *eternal damnation*, D&C 19:4-13.)

Note 3.   The term *life and damnation* are used for convenience and in a general sense to indicate the fate of the whole of mankind in the resurrection.   Strictly speaking they are the two extremes, the ultimate goal of celestial glory, which is *life* at its highest and best, and in vivid contrast therewith, the ultimate kingdom of hell.   Between these outer limits are intermediate gradations and divisions.   See "Three Degrees of Glory."

For further concerning Christ's role in bringing to pass the resurrection of mankind and eternal life for the obedient part thereof, see ATONEMENT.

Three Degrees of Glory

Objective: To show that in the resurrection there are three kingdoms or degrees of glory.

Bible:

In My Father's house are many mansions........................John 14:2...............
Glories likened to sun, moon, and stars........ ....1 Cor. 15:40-42.........
Paul tells of man caught up to third heaven...................2 Cor. 12:2................
All to be judged by works. (A reasonable inference
    is that as works vary so will rewards of glory)........Rev. 20:12................

Latter Day Scripture:

Vision of the three degrees of glory................................D&C 76...................
Vision of the celestial degree of glory..............................D&C 76:50-70..........
Vision of the terrestrial degree of glory.........................D&C 76:71-80..........
Vision of the telestial. Inherited by
    those who (in spirit would prior   D&C 76:81-90..........
    to their resurrection) suffer hell...............D&C 76:98-113........
God rules in celestial; glory excels terrestrial................D&C 76:92-95...........
Glories likened to sun, moon, and stars.......................D&C 76:96-98..........
Four kingdoms in the resurrection: three of glory,
    one not of glory. The earth to be celestial........D&C 88:17-35..........
Three degrees within the celestial glory..........................D&C 131:1-4............

Related References:

The meek shall inherit the earth......................................Matt. 5:5...................
And I saw a new heaven and a new earth.......................Rev. 21:1.................

For further concerning the celestialized earth, see "After the Millennium."   **CHRIST'S REIGN ON EARTH.**
Concerning the fate of sons of perdition, see "After the Resurrection."   HELL.

SABBATH DAY

Sunday, the True Sabbath

Objective: To show that Christ's resurrection on the first day of the week marked the beginning of Christian observance of Sunday — called the Lord's day — which latter day revelation has reaffirmed is acceptable as the day for worship.

Bible: Bible

Christ arose on the first day. (Story setting)..............John 20:1...............
Disciples assembled on first day. (Story setting)..........John 20:19..............
Disciples met again after eight days. (Story setting)......John 20:26...............
Disciples met to break bread on the first day..................Acts 20:7...............
Collection for Saints to be made on first day.................1 Cor. 16:1-2............
John in the Spirit on the Lord's day..............................Rev. 1:10...............

Latter Day Scripture: Latter Day Scripture

This, the Lord's day. (Revelation given on Sunday)......D&C 59:9-13..........

Related References: Related References

If we are under Jewish Sabbath must we not observe all?	Death for not keeping Sabbath	Ex. 31:14-17.............
	Various Sabbaths "forever"	Lev. 23:10-43...........
	Sabbath of years commanded	Lev. 25:1-10.............

Jesus came to fulfill the law................................Matt. 5:17...............
The Sabbath was made for man. (Story setting)..........Mark 2:27-28...........
Lord of Sabbath accused of disregarding Sabbath........Luke 6:1-11............
The law was a schoolmaster to bring us to Christ.........Gal. 3:24-25............
No one to be judged in respect of Sabbath.................Col. 2:16...............
The old covenant superseded by the new....................Heb. 8:1-13...............

Note. "The Hebrew Sabbaths fell on the same dates every year. Hence *they fell on a different day of the week every year.*" Samuel Walter Gamble. *Sunday, The True Sabbath of God.*

Proper Observance of the Sabbath

Objective: To show that, more important than the question of which day in the week is the Sabbath, the Lord requires the observance of one day in seven as a day of worship, prayer, and rest.

Bible: Bible

On the seventh day God rested.............................Gen. 2:1-3...............
Remember the Sabbath day to keep it holy................Ex. 20:8-11..............
Under Mosaic law Sabbath kept on pain of death........Ex. 31:14-17............
The seventh day shall be to you an holy day.............Ex. 35:1-3..............

Is it lawful on the Sabbath days to do good?..................Luke 6:1-11................

Jesus shows it is right to do good on Sabbath..............Luke 13:11-17...........

Jesus heals on Sabbath, and Jews seek His life...........John 5:1-18...............

Latter Day Scripture: **Latter Day Scripture**

How the Lord's day should be observed........................D&C 59:9-13...........

Related References: **Related References**

_____

_____

_____

_____

SACRAMENT OF THE LORD'S SUPPER

Objective: To show that the sacrament of the Lord's supper was instituted by the Savior as an emblem of His atonement, and the partaking of it by the Church denotes the acceptance of His sacrifice, the pledge to always remember Him, and the covenant to obey His commandments — in compliance with which the Lord promises the abiding influence of His Spirit.

Bible: **Bible**

Lord's supper instituted. (Story setting)........................Matt. 26:26-30.........

This do in remembrance of Me. (Story setting)...........Luke 22:15-20............

Sacrament foreshadowed. "He that eateth My flesh"....John 6:50-54..............

The Lord's supper observed by early Church................Acts 2:46....................

Disciples met to break bread on the first day................Acts 20:7..................

The sacrament termed the "Lord's supper"..................1 Cor. 11:20.............

Not for unworthy. "For this cause many are weak"......1 Cor. 11:23-24.........

Latter Day Scripture: **Latter Day Scripture**

Lord's supper instituted among Nephites......................3 Nephi 18:1-12.......

None to partake of flesh and blood unworthily..............3 Nephi 18:27-32.....

Sacramental prayers for bread and wine......................Moroni Chaps. 4-5...

Sacramental prayers for bread and wine......................D&C 20:75-79..........

Authority given for use of water. (Story setting)..........D&C 27:1-4................

Trespassers not to partake of sacrament........................D&C 46:4-5................

Related References: **Related References**

Israel's Passover. (Story setting.) A type of
    Christ's sacrifice. (Compare 1 Cor. 5:7)...............Ex. 12:12-14..........

_____

_____

_____

_____

SALVATION FOR THE DEAD
Baptism Required of All

Objective: To introduce the doctrine of baptism for the dead by showing, first that baptism is binding, without exception, upon all mankind.

Bible: Bible

He that believeth and is baptized shall be saved............Mark 16:15-16.........
Born of water and of the Spirit. (Story setting)...........John 3:5................

Latter Day Scripture   Latter Day Scripture

Men must be baptized or be damned...............................2 Nephi 9:23-24.......

Related References: Related References

Salvation in Christ's name. (Story setting)..................Acts 4:12...............

See also "Essential to Salvation." BAPTISM.

Gospel Preached to the Dead by Christ

Objective: To show that Christ preached the gospel in the world of departed spirits, notwithstanding the fact that His hearers could not be saved without baptism.

Bible: Bible

Prisoners in pit; after many days to be visited. ⎰Isa. 24:22..................
  (May refer to Jesus' delivery of captive spirits)...... ⎱Isa. 42:6-7...........
Today shalt thou be in Paradise. (Story setting)..........Luke 23:42-43...........
Jesus "not yet ascended." (Story setting)....................John 20:15-17..........
Christ preached to the spirits in prison...........................1 Pet. 3:18-20..........
The gospel preached also to them that are dead...........1 Pet. 4:6..............

Latter Day Scripture: Latter Day Scripture

Spirits visited by Son inherit terrestrial glory.................D&C 76:71-73........
Wicked of Noah's time in torment till Christ's day........PGP, Moses 7:38-39
Enoch foresees redemption of spirits in prison..............PGP, Moses 7:55-57

Related References: Related References

Thou wilt not leave my soul in hell..................Psalm 16:9-11............
The dead shall hear the voice.................................John 5:25-29............
Lord both of the dead and the living........................Rom. 14:9...............
If in this life only we have hope in Christ...................1 Cor. 15:19...........
Every knee to bow in heaven, earth, and under earth....Philip. 2:9-11.........
No punishment for those without the law.....................2 Nephi 9:25-27...
Those in prison to be redeemed..D&C 88:99..............

See also HELL and HEREAFTER.

Baptism for the Dead

Objective: To show that the righteous dead may receive effective baptism performed in their behalf by properly authorized persons on earth.

Bible:	Bible
I will send you Elijah the Prophet. (Chapter)..............Mal. 4:5-6*...............	
Why are they then baptized for the dead?.....................1 Cor. 15:29..............	

Latter Day Scripture:	Latter Day Scripture
Elijah restores keys of work for the dead......................D&C 110:13-16*.......	
Baptisms for dead to be performed in temple..................D&C 124:39.............	
Salvation for the dead explained................................D&C 128....................	

Related References:	Related References
Saviors shall come upon Mount Zion............................Obad. 1:21...............	
They without us cannot be made perfect.....................Heb. 11:40...............	

Note 1.   To assert that all who have died have already been consigned to an *everlasting* state of heaven or hell (and no amount of effort on their part can change their status) is to assume that they are judged before the day of judgment, *which the scriptures affirm, is yet future.* (Rev. 20.)   See JUDGMENT.

Note 2.   Jews sought boastfully to trace their genealogy to Abraham as evidence that they were the elect of God.   It was such pointless genealogies that Paul wished Saints to disregard in Titus chapter 3, verse 9.   Compare Matt. 3:9; Gal. 3:29.

SECOND COMING OF JESUS CHRIST

Christ's Coming Foretold

Objective: To show that the glorious second coming of Jesus Christ is "near, even at the doors" and that it will be attended by catastrophic disturbances in nature, destruction of the wicked, and resurrection of the righteous dead.

Bible:	Bible
He shall stand at the latter day upon the earth..............Job 19:25-27..............	
Our God shall come. Saints gathered together.............Psalm 50:3-6.............	
Howl ye, for the day of the Lord is at hand...................Isa. 13:6-14...............	
The earth shall reel to and fro. (Chapter).....................Isa. 24:20.................	
All flesh shall see the glory of the Lord........................Isa. 40:3-5...	
War of "all nations" fought at Jerusalem. Lord to appear on Mt. of Olives. (Also Zech. 13:6)..........Zech. 14:1-9*.............	
Who may abide the day of His coming?.........................Mal. 3:1-5.................	
Day, hour unknown; as in days of Noah. (Chapter)....Matt. 24:29-51†........	
Hereafter shall ye see the Son of Man. (Story)............Matt. 26:64................	
Then shall they see the Son of Man coming..................Luke 21:25-28............	
Jesus to return as He went. "Ye men of Galilee".........Acts 1:9-11................	
He shall send Jesus Christ. (Story setting)..................Acts 3:19-21..............	

Righteous to be caught up. Dead to rise........................1 Thess. 4:13-17.......
Lord to come as a thief in the night................................1 Thess. 5:1-6............
Lord shall come to be glorified in His Saints.................2 Thess. 1:7-10..........
Lord to come as a thief. A day of burning. (Chapter)....2 Pet. 3:10...............
Enoch's prophecy: "The Lord cometh"......................Jude 14-15.................
He cometh with clouds. Every eye shall see Him........Rev. 1:7....................
The wicked to call on mountains to fall on them............Rev. 6:12-17..............
144,000 to stand on Mt. Zion. (Compare Rev. 7:4-9).....Rev. 14:1‡§..........
Thunder, hail, and greatest earthquake in history..........Rev. 16:15-21............
Resurrection of the righteous. Satan to be bound........Rev. 20:1-6.........

Latter Day Scripture: Latter Day Scripture

Fall of the abominable church. Righteous preserved.....1 Nephi 22:13-24.....
Christ's visit to the Nephites. (A dramatic   ⎰3 Nephi 8:5-25.........
    foreshadowing of the coming yet future).................⎱3 Nephi 11:1-17.......
Those not heeding apostles, prophets, to be cut off.......D&C 1:11-14............
Wicked to be burned by fire. Righteous dead to rise.......D&C 29:9-13.........
Nature in fury to declare repentance at Coming............D&C 43:17-29.........
The Saints that have slept shall come forth..................D&C 45:44-46*......
Jesus to display wounds on Mount. Satan bound..........D&C 45:47-55*.........
He cometh not as a woman. Mts. to be made low........D&C 49:22-23.........
144,000 high priests sealed, 12,000 of each tribe............D&C 77:11‡.........
A new song to be sung. Millennial era heralded.............D&C 84:96-102.......
A great sign. Saints quickened. Details told................D&C 88:86-110......
All shall see Lord. Corruptible things burned................D&C 101:22-25.......
Great day of the Lord near, even at the doors................D&C 110:13-16........
Joseph Smith not told time of Coming. His prayer.....D&C 130:14-17.........
144,000 to stand on Mt. Zion. (Compare D&C 84:2).....D&C 133:16-19§......
Ocean to be driven back; continents made one.............D&C 133:20-25........
Christ's glory to obscure sun. Saints to rise.................D&C 133:45-56.......
City of Enoch to return. The thousand years.............PGP, Moses 7:60-66
Inspired translation of the 24th chapter of Matthew......PofGP, Smith 1†.....
They that come shall burn them. (Story setting)..........PGP, Smith 2:37.....

Related References: Related References

Parable of the ten virgins. (Compare D&C 45:46-59).....Matt. 25:1-13............
Put on whole armour of God to withstand the evil day....D&C 27:15-18..........
Cry repentance, preparing the way of the Lord.............D&C 34:6-12...........
Go forth baptizing with water, preparing the way..........D&C 39:19-24.........
Be subject to the powers that be until He reigns............D&C 58:21-22..........
Be of good cheer. Be watchful. Pray always................D&C 61:36-39..........
He that is tithed shall not be burned at Coming............D&C 64:23-25.........

Concerning conditions upon the earth following Christ's coming, see "The Millennium."
CHRIST'S REIGN ON EARTH.

Concerning the partial judgment of mankind at the coming of Christ, see "Judgment at
Christ's Coming." JUDGMENT.

Events to Precede Christ's Coming

Objective: To show that: (a) certain great events have been prophesied to transpire before Christ's coming; (b) in the midst of the tribulations of prophecy the Saints may find peace and comfort through obedience to the commandments of God.

Bible: **Bible**

When Lord shall build Zion He shall appear	Psalm 102:16*
Ancient of days (Adam) to hold grand council. (An event to prepare Saints for the Coming; see *Teachings of the Prophet Joseph Smith*, p. 157)	Dan. 7:9-14, 27†
War of "all nations" to be fought at Jerusalem	Zech. 14:1-4
A temple to be ready for the Lord. (Also vs. 2-5)	Mal. 3:1
I will send you Elijah the prophet. (Chapter)	Mal. 4:5-6‡
Gospel preached to the world. Many signs told	Matt. Chap. 24§
Men to ask, "Where is the promise of His coming?"	2 Pet. 3:1-4
Two prophets to be martyred in Jerusalem	Rev. 11:1-15‖
Armageddon, a great earthquake, hail. (Chapter)	Rev. 16:15-21

Latter Day Scripture: **Latter Day Scripture**

Peace taken away. Lord to reign over Saints	D&C 1:34-36
A desolating scourge shall go forth	D&C 5:19-20
Tribulations told: a hailstorm, flies, maggots	D&C 29:14-21
Signs of the Coming as told ancient apostles	D&C 45:26-43
Every man to be against neighbor or flee to Zion	D&C 45:63-71
No flesh shall be safe upon the waters	D&C 61:14-16
Saints to gather to Zion as wars decreed abroad	D&C 63:33-37
Two prophets to be martyred in Jerusalem	D&C 77:15‖
New Jerusalem and temple to be built	D&C 84:2-5
Desolation of abomination in the last days	D&C 84:117-120
Consumption decreed to make an end of all nations	D&C 87:6-8
Vengeance cometh speedily. How Zion may escape	D&C 97:21-26
Elijah comes. Lord's coming "at the doors"	D&C 110:13-16‡
Wrath to be poured out. Refuge in Zion's stakes	D&C 115:4-6
Adam to hold council at Adam-ondi-Ahman	D&C 116†
Israel to gather to Zion and Jerusalem	D&C 133:6-15
Ten tribes to return. (As part of the prophesied gathering of Israel this event is *presumed* to occur before the second coming)	D&C 133:26-34
City of Zion to be built. Elect to be gathered to it	PGP, Moses 7:60-66
Inspired translation of the 24th chapter of Matthew	PofGP, Smith 1§
Great judgments to come in this generation	PofGP, Smith 2:45

Related References: **Related References**

Note. "Judah must return, Jerusalem must be rebuilt, and the temple, and water come out from under the temple, and the waters of the Dead Sea be healed . . . . and all this must be done before the Son of Man will make His appearance." *Teachings of the Prophet Joseph Smith*, pp. 286-7.

SPIRITUAL GIFTS

Characteristic of Christ's Church

Objective: To show that the Church of Jesus Christ is characterized by "the gift of tongues, prophecy, revelation, visions, healing, interpretation of tongues, etc."

Bible: **Bible**

These signs shall follow them that believe....................Mark 16:17-18.........
The speaking in tongues on Pentecost. (Chapter)........Acts 2:4-8................
The Spirit is to be poured out upon all flesh in the last
    days. (Story setting.) (Also Joel 2:28-32)....Acts 2:17..................
The Lord speaks to Paul by revelation...........................Acts 9:1-9................
The Lord speaks to Ananias in a vision..........................Acts 9:10-12............
Cornelius and Peter receive visions. (Chapter)............Acts 10:1-18.............
Lord speaks to Paul in a vision. (Story setting)..........Acts 18:9................
The gift of tongues and prophecy. (Story setting)........Acts 19:6...............
Agabus prophesies Paul's fate. (Story setting).............Acts 21:10-12...........
Paul comforted by a vision. (Story setting).................Acts 23:11...............
An angel appears to Paul. (Story setting)....................Acts 27:21-26.........
Now concerning spiritual gifts. "To one is given".........1 Cor. 12:1-11...........
God hath set in the Church prophets, miracles...............1 Cor. 12:27-28.........
Tongues not given to confuse. A greater gift...............1 Cor. Chap. 14........
Paul prays Saints may have spirit of revelation............Eph. 1:15-17............
Quench not the Spirit. Despise not prophesyings..........1 Thess. 5:19-20........
The Revelation of Jesus Christ...Rev. 1:1.........,........
The testimony of Jesus is the spirit of prophecy...........Rev. 19:10................

Latter Day Scripture: **Latter Day Scripture**

Nephites blessed with prophecy and other gifts............Alma 9:21................
Woe to those who deny or spurn miraculous gifts.........3 Nephi 29:5-7.........
Spiritual gifts enumerated by Moroni...........................Moroni 10:8-19.........
Spiritual gifts are lost only through unbelief.................Moroni 10:23-25.......
Purpose and kinds of spiritual gifts.............................D&C 46:8-29..........
Signs to follow them that believe.................................D&C 84:64-72.........
President of the Church entitled to all the gifts.............D&C 107:91-92.........

Related References: **Related References**

He that believeth shall do greater works........................John 14:12.............
Book to come forth in day when miracles doubted.......Mormon 8:26............

See also LATTER DAY REVELATION.

Healing

Objective: To show that the healing of the sick is one of the gifts of Christ's Church and is (usually) performed by the laying on of hands.

Bible: Bible

Come and lay thy hand upon her. (Story setting)........Matt. 9:18................
Christ gives Twelve power to heal sickness......................Mark 3:14-15............
He laid His hands on a few sick. (Story setting).........Mark 6:5...................
They annointed the sick with oil. (Story setting).......Mark 6:13................
Jesus puts hands on blind man and heals him..............Mark 8:22-26............
They shall lay hands on the sick.................................Mark 16:17-18.........
He laid His hands on every one of them.....................Luke 4:40................
He laid His hands on her. (Story setting)...................Luke 13:11-13............
Peter orders cripple to walk. (Story setting)...............Acts 3:1-8.................
Wonders wrought by the hands of the apostles..............Acts 5:12.................
Ananias puts hands on Paul. (Story setting)...............Acts 9:17-18.............
"Stand upright on thy feet." (Story setting)...............Acts 14:8-10.............
Paul lays hands on Publius. (Story setting)................Acts 28:8.................
Is any sick among you? Let him call for elders...........James 5:14-15............

Latter Day Scripture: Latter Day Scripture

Zeezrom healed by Alma in the land of Sidom..............Alma 15:1-12............
Nephi raises brother from dead. (Story setting)...........3 Nephi 7:19-20.......
Savior heals Nephite sick. (Story setting)...................3 Nephi 17:9-10........
Healings etc. to be performed only on request..............D&C 24:13-14...........
Elders to lay hands on sick. Faith necessary...............D&C 42:43-48..........

Related References: Related References

Sick not always healed. Paul had in-
  firmities. (Also 1 Cor. 11:30; 2 Tim.
  4:20; Heb. 9:27; D&C 42:43-48)........................2 Cor. 12:7-9.............

Miracles Alone Not Proof of True Church

Objective: To show that miraculous displays indicate but do not by themselves establish that a church is of Christ, as the devil is capable of producing counterfeit gifts.

Bible: Bible

Pharaoh's magicians duplicate Moses' miracles..............Ex. 7:10-22..............
Many (false) prophets to be cast out at judgment........Matt. 7:21-23............
There shall be false Christs and prophets.....................Matt. 24:24.............
Satan transformed into an angel of light....................2 Cor. 11:13-15.........
A wicked one to work miracles and be consumed..........2 Thess. 2:8-9............
They are the spirits of devils working miracles.............Rev. 16:13-15............

Latter Day Scripture: **Latter Day Scripture**

  The devil came to Korihor as an angel. (Story setting)....Alma 30:53...............
There are many false spirits abroad in the earth...........D&C 50:2-3.............
Devil comes to Joseph Smith as an angel of light.........D&C 128:20.............
The devil appears to Moses. (Chapter).........................PGP, Moses 1:12-23

Related References: **Related References**

  Spiritualist mediums disapproved. To
    seek them is wrong. (Also 1 Sam.   ⌠Lev. 19:31................
    28:6-7; 1 Chron. 10:13; Isa. 8:19-20)....................⌊Lev. 20:6..................

See also "Unauthorized Acts Not Recognized by God." AUTHORITY IN THE MINISTRY.

TITHES AND OFFERINGS

Objective: To show that tithing is a divine law of ancient origin restored to earth in these latter days.

Bible: **Bible**

  Abraham pays tithes. (Story setting)...........................Gen. 14:18-20...........
Jacob vows to pay tenth to Lord. (Story setting)........Gen. 28:20-22............
Moses' instructions on tithing...Lev. 27:30-34...........
"Will a man rob God?" Tithe payers blessed................Mal. 3:8-12...............
Tithing should not be neglected. (Story setting).........Luke 11:42...............
Before the time of Moses, Abraham paid tithes............Heb. 7:1-10...............

Latter Day Scripture: **Latter Day Scripture**

  He that is tithed shall not be burned at Coming...........D&C 64:23...............
The restored law of tithing...D&C 119..................

Related References: **Related References**

  Only gifts given freely are acceptable. Cain and Abel....Gen. 4:3-7.................
Honor Lord with substance; barns to be filled...............Prov. 3:9-10.............
Lay not up for yourselves treasures upon earth...........Matt. 6:19-21...........
The higher law of consecration had among Nephites........4 Nephi 1:3, 15-18....

TRANSGRESSION AND THE FALL

Objective: To show that the fall of Adam and Eve was a necessary change from an unmortal state to a condition of mortality in order to provide mortal parentage for the spirit children of God who were ready and waiting for the experience of earth life.

Bible: **Bible**

Adam told that if he ate fruit he
   would surely die. (He was not
   subject to death until the fall)........................Gen. 2:15-17*............
The fall and expulsion from the Garden of Eden............Gen. Chap. 3............
By one man sin entered world and death by sin............Rom. 5:12................
As in Adam all die, in Christ all made alive..................1 Cor. 15:21-22..........
The serpent beguiled Eve through his subtlety.............2 Cor. 11:3................
The woman deceived; to be saved in childbearing........1 Tim. 2:14-15..........

Latter Day Scripture: **Latter Day Scripture**

Opposition and the fall. Life a probation......................2 Nephi 2:14-21.......
Adam and Eve fell from a state in which
   they would have lived forever in
   order "that men might be" (mortal)......................2 Nephi 2:22-26*.....
Death passed on all. A power of resurrection...............2 Nephi 9:6................
Cherubim and a flaming sword. (Story setting)............Alma 12:20-37..........
The fall and atonement discussed by Alma....................Alma Chap. 42..........
Spiritual death brought by transgression.....................D&C 29:40-45..........
Every spirit of man innocent in beginning....................D&C 93:38...............
Moses' account of fall as revealed to Joseph Smith........PGP, Moses 4:5-31..
Except for the fall men would not have been born..........PGP, Moses 5:10-11
"Because that Adam fell we are"...................................PGP, Moses 6:48.....

Related References: **Related References**

The fall foreseen. Christ the foreordained SAVIOR......1 Pet. 1:18-20............
Sin is transgression of law. (Also Rom. 4:15)...............1 John 3:4................
Adam also known as Ancient of Days, Michael.............D&C 27:11...............
Adam a prince over the human race forever...................D&C 107:53-56........

Note. "Here let me say that therein consisted the fall — the eating of things unfit, the taking into the body of the things that made of that body a thing of earth; and I take this occasion to raise my voice against the false interpretation of scripture, which has been adopted by certain people, and is current in their minds, and is referred to in a hushed and half-secret way, that the fall of man consisted in some offense against the laws of chastity and of virtue. Such a doctrine is abomination. What right have we to turn the scriptures from their proper sense and meaning? What right have we to declare that God meant not what He said? The fall was a natural process, resulting through the incorporation into the bodies of our first parents of the things that came from food unfit, through the violation of the command of God regarding what they should eat." James E. Talmage, *Jesus the Christ*, p. 30.

URIM AND THUMMIM

Objective: To show that Joseph Smith's claim concerning the possession and use of the Urim and Thummim is in full harmony with the testimony of scripture.

Bible: **Bible**

    Ephod, breastplate, Urim and Thummim......................Ex. Chap. 28...........

    Urim and Thummim put in breastplate.........................Lev. 8:7-8...............

    Counsel gained "after the judgment of Urim"...............Num. 27:21...............

    No answer given through Urim. (Story setting)...........1 Sam. 28:6..............

    Bring me hither the ephod. (Story setting)..................1 Sam. 30:7-8..........

    A priest with Urim and with Thummim.......................Ezra 2:62-63............

Latter Day Scripture: **Latter Day Scripture**

    "Interpreters" and seership. (Story setting)................Mosiah 8:13-18..........

    Mosiah translates by means of "two stones".................Mosiah 28:13-16.......

    Two stones will I give. (Story setting).........................Ether 3:22-23...........

    Abraham studies stars by Urim and Thummim.............PofGP, Abrm. 3:1-4

    Urim and Thummim with plates. (Story setting).........PofGP, Smith 2:35..

    Urim and Thummim obtained. (Story setting).............Pof GP, Smith 2:59..

Related References: **Related References**

    Celestialized earth to be used as Urim and Thummim....D&C 130:8-11...........

WORD OF WISDOM

Objective: To show that the Word of Wisdom is a restored law of health which, in its essential aspects, was understood and observed by the Children of Israel anciently.

Bible: **Bible**

    Fruits of field to be used for meat..................................Gen. 1:29.....................

    Thou shalt eat the herb of the field...............................Gen. 3:18.....................

    Herbs and meat to be used by man................................Gen. 9:2-3...................

    Israelites allowed to eat only certain meats...................Deut. 14:3-20.............

    Neither let her drink wine. (Story setting)..................Judges 13:13-14........

    Wine is a mocker, strong drink is raging.......................Prov. 20:1...................

    Look not thou upon the wine.......................................Prov. 23:31-35..........

    Woe to those that follow strong drink............................Isa. 5:11-12...............

    Boys refuse rich foods; become king's advisors.............Dan. Chap. 1............

    Babylon falls in night of drinking and revelry................Dan. Chap. 5.............

    Ye are the temple of God..1 Cor. 3:16-17...........

    Be not drunk with wine...Eph. 5:18...................

    Bishops not to be given to wine....................................Titus 1:7...................

Latter Day Scripture   **Latter Day Scripture**

Nephites drug Lamanites with wine and escape............Mosiah Chap. 22......
Lamanite guards made drunk. A Nephite victory........Alma Chap. 55..........
Shared outwits drunken army. (Story setting).............Ether 14:5-6..............
Retire to bed early and arise early.................................D&C 88:124.............
The Word of Wisdom. A revealed law of health..........D&C 89....................

Related References: **Related References**

God's laws (in the final analysis) are spiritual...............D&C 29:34...............

APPENDIX

Note 1

THE PREMORTAL GODSHIP OF CHRIST

"We claim scriptural authority for the assertion that Jesus Christ was and is God the Creator, the God who revealed Himself to Adam, Enoch, and all the antediluvial patriarchs and prophets down to Noah; the God of Abraham, Isaac and Jacob; the God of Israel as a united people, and the God of Ephraim and Judah after the disruption of the Hebrew nation; the God who made Himself known to the prophets from Moses to Malachi; the God of the Old Testament record; and the God of the Nephites. We affirm that Jesus Christ was and is Jehovah, the Eternal One." (JESUS THE CHRIST, James E. Talmage, Chap. 4, p. 32.)

Note 2

A Condensation of

THE FATHER AND THE SON: A DOCTRINAL EXPOSITION

by the

FIRST PRESIDENCY AND THE TWELVE

God the Eternal Father, whom we designate by the exalted name-title "Elohim," is the literal Parent of our Lord and Savior Jesus Christ, and of the spirits of the human race. Elohim is the Father in every sense in which Jesus Christ is so designated, and distinctively He is the Father of spirits.

Jesus Christ applies to Himself both titles, "Son" and "Father." Indeed, He specifically said to the brother of Jared: "Behold, I am Jesus Christ. I am the Father and the Son" (Ether 3:14). Jesus Christ is the Son of Elohim both as spiritual and bodily offspring; that is to say, Elohim is literally the Father of the spirit of Jesus Christ and also of the body in which Jesus Christ performed His mission in the flesh, and which body died on the cross and was afterward taken up by the process of resurrection, and is now the immortalized tabernacle of the eternal spirit of our Lord and Savior.

Jesus Christ as "Father"

The "Father" as "Creator." Scriptures that refer to God in any way as the Father of the heavens and the earth are to be understood as signifying that God is the Maker, the Organizer, the Creator of the heavens and the earth. With this meaning, as the context shows in every case, Jehovah, who is Jesus Christ the Son of Elohim, is called "the Father," and even "the very eternal Father of heaven and of earth" [Ether 4:7; see also Alma 11:38, 39 and Mosiah 15:4 and 16:15.] With analogous meaning Jesus Christ is called "The Everlasting Father" (Isaiah 9:6; compare 2 Nephi 19:6). The descriptive titles "Everlasting" and "Eternal" in the foregoing texts are synonymous.

That Jesus Christ, whom we also know as Jehovah, was the executive of the Father, Elohim, in the work of creation is set forth in the book *Jesus the Christ*, chapter 4. Jesus Christ, being the Creator, is consistently called the Father of heaven and earth in the sense explained above; and since His creations are of eternal quality He is very properly called the Eternal Father of heaven and earth.

Jesus Christ the "Father" of Those Who Abide in His Gospel — Salvation is attainable only through compliance with the laws and ordinances of the Gospel; and all who are thus saved become sons and daughters unto God in a distinctive sense. In a revelation given through Joseph the Prophet to Emma Smith the Lord Jesus addressed the woman as "My daughter," and said: "for verily I say unto you, all those who receive my gospel are sons and daughters in my kingdom" (D. & C. 25:1). In many instances the Lord has addressed men as His sons (e.g. D. & C. 9:1; 34:3; 121:7).

That by obedience to the Gospel men may become sons of God, both as sons of Jesus Christ, and, through Him, as sons of His Father, is set forth in many revelations given in the current dispensation. To Orson Pratt the Lord spoke through Joseph the Seer, in 1830: "My son Orson, hearken and hear and behold what I, the Lord God, shall say unto you, even Jesus Christ your Redeemer; the light and the life of the world; a light which shineth in darkness and the darkness comprehendeth it not; Who so loved the world that he gave his own life, that as many as would believe might become the sons of God. Wherefore you are my son" (D. & C. 34:1-3). Consider also the following given in 1831: "Hearken and listen to the voice of him who is from all eternity to all eternity, the Great I Am, even Jesus Christ — The light and the life of the world; a light which shineth in darkness and the darkness comprehendeth it not; The same which came in the meridian of time unto mine own, and mine own received me not; But to as many as received me, gave I power to become my sons; and even so will I give unto as many as will receive me, power to become my sons" (D. & C. 39:1-4).

In tragic contrast with the blessed state of those who become children of God through obedience to the Gospel of Jesus Christ is that of the unregenerate, who are specifically called the children of the devil. Note the words of Christ, while in the flesh, to certain wicked Jews who boasted of their Abrahamic lineage: "If ye were Abraham's children, ye would do the works of Abraham. * * * Ye do the deeds of your father * * * If God were your Father, ye would love me. * * * Ye are of your father the devil, and the lusts of your father ye will do" (John 8:39, 41, 42, 44). Thus Satan is designated as the father of the wicked though we cannot assume any personal relationship of parent and children as existing between him and them. A combined illustration showing that the righteous are the children of God and the wicked the children of the devil appears in the parable of the Tares: "The good seed are the children of the kingdom; but the tares are the children of the wicked one" (Matt. 13:38).

By the new birth — that of water and the Spirit — mankind may become children of Jesus Christ, being through the means by Him provided "begotten sons and daughters unto God" (D. & C. 76:24). If it be proper to speak of those who accept and abide in the Gospel as Christ's sons and daughters — and upon this matter the scriptures are explicit and cannot be gainsaid nor denied — it is consistently proper to speak of Jesus Christ as the Father of the righteous, they having become His children and He having been made their Father through the second birth — the baptismal regeneration.

Jesus Christ the "Father" by Divine Investiture of Authority — In all His dealings with the human family Jesus the Son has represented and yet represents Elohim His Father in power and authority. This is true of Christ in His pre-existent, antemortal, or unembodied state, in the which he was known as Jehovah; also during his embodiment in the flesh; and during His labors as a disembodied spirit in the realm of the dead; and since that period in His resurrected state. To the Jews He said: "I and my Father are one" (John 10:30; see also 17:11, 22); yet He declared "My Father is greater than I" (John 14:28); and further, "I am come in my Father's name" (John 5:43; see also 10:25). The same truth was declared by Christ Himself to the Nephites (see 3 Nephi 20:35 and 28:10), and has been reaffirmed by revelation in the present dispensation (D. & C. 50:43). Thus the Father placed His name upon the Son; and Jesus Christ spoke and ministered in and through the Father's name; and so far as power, authority, and Godship are concerned His words and acts were and are those of the Father.

The ancient apostle, John, was visited by an angel who ministered and spoke in the name of Jesus Christ. As we read: "The Revelation of Jesus Christ, which God gave unto him, to shew unto his servants things which must shortly come to pass; and he sent and signified it by his angel unto his servant John" (Revelation 1:1). John was about to worship the angelic being who spoke in the name of the Lord Jesus Christ, but was forbidden: "And I John saw these things, and heard them. And when I had heard and seen, I fell down to worship before the feet of the angel which shewed me these things. Then saith he unto me, See thou do it not; for I am thy fellowservant, and of thy brethren the prophets, and of them which keep the sayings of this book: worship God" (Rev. 22:8, 9). And then the angel continued to speak as though he were the Lord Himself: "And, behold, I come quickly; and my reward is with me, to give every man according as his work shall be. I am Alpha and Omega, the beginning and the end, the first and the last" (verses 12, 13). The resurrected Lord, Jesus Christ, who had been exalted to the right hand of God His Father, had placed His name upon the angel sent to John, and the angel spoke in the first person, saying "I come quickly." "I am Alpha and Omega," though he meant that Jesus Christ would come, and that Jesus Christ was Alpha and Omega. (For the complete unabridged statement by The First Presidency and The Twelve see *Articles of Faith*, James E. Talmage, Appendix 2, pp. 465-473.)